My name is **Robert Hayes-McCoy**. I'm a professional copywriter for the direct marketing and direct mail industry. My speciality is writing sales letters for large and small businesses, government agencies and charities.

It's my job to persuade people to buy or use the products and services offered by my clients. And if the number of national and international awards that my sales campaigns have won is anything to go by I guess you could say that I write more persuasive sales letters than most.

So much so that, over the years, my sales letters, fundraising letters and direct mail letters have won numerous 'best of' awards. These include the **Best of America Echo Awards**, **Best of Europe FEDMA Awards** and **Best of Ireland Awards for Excellence** for direct marketing and copywriting. In addition, I have been awarded many 'special category' national and international awards and accolades for my copywriting and direct marketing abilities.

I also run seminars and workshops to train people how to write their own persuasive sales letters and I've spoken on the subject of writing sales letters at many different national and international marketing conferences and events.

Over the years, I've seen simply tens of thousands of different sales letters. And the one thing that has never ceased to amaze me is how poorly written many of these letters are. Quite simply, they are not persuasive enough!

By this I mean they are not strong enough to hold their readers' attention, arouse their interest and create an active desire in their minds to take immediate action!

Poorly-written business letters like these are hugely wasteful. They needlessly squander new business- and income-generating opportunities. They are also a crying shame. They're a shame because, with just a little bit more knowledge and understanding of some of the secrets of the professional copywriter's trade, most people could write really great sales letters. And this is exactly what this book is all about.

It's about showing YOU in the most enjoyable and painless way possible how to write ... **Persuasive Business Letters That Really Sell!**

PERSUASIVE
DIRECT MARKETING

Here's what you say and how you write it!

International Award-winning Copywriter

Robert Hayes-McCoy

www.oaktreepress.com

OAK TREE PRESS
19 Rutland Street, Cork, Ireland
www.oaktreepress.com

A catalogue record of this book is
available from the British Library.

ISBN 1-86076-294-8

Printed in Ireland by Colour Books.

CONTENTS

THE BEGINNING

'Where shall I begin, please your Majesty', he asked. 'Begin at the beginning', the King said, gravely, 'and go on till you come to the end: then stop'.
Lewis Carroll, *Alice's Adventures in Wonderland* (1865), Ch.12.

Welcome to my book! The wonderful thing about this book is that, by the time you finish it, I can promise you that you will be armed with all the information you need to write very persuasive sales letters. But before you go any further, let me tell you a story.

A foreign-born plumber living in New York wrote to the Bureau of Standards in Washington to say that he found hydrochloric acid fine for cleaning drains: did they agree?

Washington replied, 'The efficacy of hydrochloric is indisputable but the chlorine residue is incompatible with metallic permanence'.

The plumber wrote back, 'I'm mighty glad to find that you agree with me'.

Considerably alarmed, the Bureau replied immediately, 'We cannot assume responsibility for the production of toxic and noxious residues with hydrochloric acid, and suggest that you use an alternative procedure'.

The plumber replied, 'I'm happy to learn that you still agree with me'.

Whereupon Washington, in desperation, replied, 'STOP! Don't use hydrochloric acid ... IT EATS THE HELL OUT OF PIPES!'

What's happening in this little story? What's happening is that two people are writing to each other in English, but they are failing absolutely to communicate with each other. You see the English language used by the Bureau of Standards in Washington is totally beyond the plumber's comprehension. And it's only when Washington eventually talks to the plumber in the kind of plain English that he understands that the message, finally, gets through.

This is what often happens in sales letters. People sit down and pick up their pen, or pull out their keyboard, all ready to write an important sales letter and something weird happens.

They start writing things like *'I beg to refer to your letter of the 16th ultimo'*, or *'herewith is the information that you requested'*.

Strange, archaic and wonderful words pour out of 'the pen'. Words that people would never dream of saying in everyday conversation because they sound downright corny. And yet, for some very odd reason, normal sane people will happily use these words in their written communications.

Dear Sir / Madam

I refer to your correspondence of 'even date' and beg to inform you that the item, which you so kindly requested, is ... ' *YUCK!*

Okay! This example is a bit over the top. But you can see why my immediate reaction is to say ... *'Yuck!'*. It all sounds like something that came out of the Ark.

What I am going to tell you about in this book is how to create business letters that:

◊   People understand

◊   Are really easy to write

◊   People enjoy reading

◊   Are hard to leave down

◊   Are good to look at ... and

◊   Sell YOU – the writer – and your products and services at the same time!

In a nutshell, MAGIC LETTERS!

1. Getting Started with Magic

> 'Beware the Jabberwock, my son!
> **The jaws that bite, the claws that catch.'**
> Lewis Carroll, *Through The Looking Glass* (1872), Ch.1.

There are a number of tried, tested and proven words that have the ability to capture most readers' attention right at the very start of a sales letter. These are 'magic words'.

Time and time again, you will find them appearing, reappearing and featuring yet again, in the most successful sales letters of all. That's because these words are 'hidden persuaders'. There's only about a dozen of them. They are simple to learn and easy to remember. And I'm now going to tell you what they are.

Furthermore, as I take you through each one of them, you'll begin to see that they all have something very basic in common. And once you understand what they have in common, you're already well on your way to writing very persuasive sales letters.

But before we enter into this magic world of mine, let me warn you that you may decide, before you are even half-way through your journey, that you can't possibly use some of these words with your own customers and clients. There may be all kinds of reasons for this. For example: you may decide that some of them are just that little bit too close to 'junk mail words' for your liking.

But it's essential from the outset that you become familiar with these words and – **more importantly** – understand what is it that makes them so universally popular. Because once you know this,

I'll be very surprised if you cannot harness the persuasive selling powers of at least one of these words and use it to your own advantage.

Now, let me take each of the magic words in no particular order of priority and let me explain to you why they work so successfully in written communications ... particularly in the opening sentence or in the headline of a letter.

LET'S START WITH A WINNER!

The first word that I want to talk to you about is the word 'WIN'. Everybody likes to win something. So powerful is the word 'win' that, if you think about it, Las Vegas would probably NEVER exist without it. Win is a very short word. It's easy to say, it's easy to write and everybody knows exactly what it means.

It's also a very greedy word.

By this, I mean I would love you to 'win' the Lotto! You are obviously a lovely person, because you purchased my book, and wouldn't it be fabulous if you won a million Euro in the Lotto, to spend exactly as you wish? I, for one, would like that to happen to you! And I certainly would be up there in the front offering you my heartiest congratulations if you won.

But do you want to know something? Although I can assure you that I still think it would be wonderful if you won the Lotto, deep – **DEEP** – down I would much prefer to win the Lotto myself! Now that would be even better! You see, I'm greedy!

So what I want you to remember is that while 'win' is a powerful word, if you want to get maximum effect from using this word in your sales letters the person who wins has to be your reader. Tell your reader up-front that he or she has won something interesting and I promise you that they will read every single word of your letter.

Never forget that 'win' is a greedy word! That's why, used correctly at the beginning of your written communications, it becomes one of the most 'attention-grabbing' words in the English language.

YOUR NEXT MAGIC WORD IS 'GUARANTEE'

A 'guarantee' is a formal promise or assurance that an obligation will be fulfilled or that something is of a specific quality and durability. Put the magic words 'guarantee' and 'win' together and something interesting begins to happen. For example, you can start sentences like ... *'I guarantee that you will win'*, or write up-beat messages like ... *'It's a winner – guaranteed!* ... Or *'Everyone is guaranteed to win!'* There are umpteen different sentences, headlines and messages that you can create using these two words: 'win' and 'guarantee'.

Can you see what I'm doing? Already, I'm taking two of the magic words and I'm beginning to create interesting sentences.

The word 'guarantee' is deceptively powerful and persuasive. It certainly is a greed-satisfying word because, in this case, it confirms beyond all doubt to your reader that he or she is going to win.

What I always tell my clients is that the smaller, or less well-known, your company or your product is, the more important it is for you to spell out, or use, the word 'guarantee' in your sales letters and promotional material.

Big-brand companies, large corporations and banks don't really have to mention the word guarantee in their promotional material. That's because it's more or less implied in their name. But if you are running a small, or medium-sized, company the word 'guarantee' can be a very important tool in your promotional toolkit.

Let me give you a little example of what I mean by this. Suppose, just suppose, that you open your newspaper tomorrow morning and you see a small 'words only' advertisement that reads:

**Invest €10,000 in this fund immediately and
you will get €20,000 back at the end of the month.**

Sounds too good to be true, doesn't it? A 100% return on your investment in a single month! Well, it gets even more incredible as you read on; because my 'pretend' ad goes on to say ...

All you have to do is send €10,000 to ABC Investors, Unit 1A, Back Lane, Higher Street, Dublin.

Uh Oh! Let's face it, would anybody in their right mind put €10,000 into an envelope and send it to a dubiously-named company with an address like this? Of course, they wouldn't.

But hold on! Wait a moment! Don't discard your newspaper just yet! Let's just say, down there at the end of the ad, there's a sentence that reads as follows:

This fund is guaranteed by the World Bank.

That would make a difference, wouldn't it?

And okay, well you might wonder what on earth the World Bank is doing in associating itself with a company that operates out of such a shady-sounding address as Unit 1A, Back Lane ... but that guarantee does make a difference, doesn't it?

Remember, I told you not to discard your newspaper just yet! Now, let's say you turn to the front page and there before you, in big bold letters, is a headline that shouts out at you:

Armed Robbery At Local Bank - Manager In Tears!

And the following day, you arrive at your local bank to collect that €10,000 that you want to invest, only to be greeted at the door by a shame-faced manager, who says:

> 'I'm terribly sorry but I've got bad news for you. You see, we had an armed robbery yesterday and the thieves stole your money! It's all gone, I'm afraid. By the way, I know it's your money that they stole, because I recognised it instantly by the way the corners were curled up. So I'm sorry, you've no money, at all, left in the bank.'

It just wouldn't happen, would it? No, not at all, that's what banks are all about, you see. They safeguard your money. Banks are BIG! So, if there's a robbery at your local branch, it really doesn't affect the security of your money. Nowadays, they don't even have to spell it out to you that the security of your money is guaranteed in their bank; it is implied in the name of the bank itself.

Big company names and major brand names enjoy a unique position of having an 'invisible' guarantee associated with their name or brand. Small, relatively-unknown companies don't have this invisible guarantee associated with them so they need to spell out a guarantee to the readers of their sales letters and promotional material.

So, if you are writing a sales letter for a relatively-unknown company, product or service, the magic word 'guarantee' will be an important item in your promotional tool-kit.

SUMMARY OF CHAPTER 1:
HERE'S WHAT YOU SAY AND HOW YOU SAY IT

☐ We live in a very busy world so, if your sales letter is to be successful, you should apply a little 'magic' to your opening paragraph to guarantee that you capture your readers' attention immediately.

☐ There are a number of tried, tested and proven words that have the ability to capture most readers' attention. These are the 'magic words'.

☐ Magic words are 'hidden persuaders'. There's only about a dozen of them. They are simple to learn and easy to remember.

☐ 'Win' and 'guarantee' are two of the most powerful magic words at your disposal.

☐ You'll find one or other of these words featuring in the opening paragraph of many successful sales letters.

2. MORE MAGIC WORDS!

> 'The rule is jam to-morrow and jam yesterday – but never jam today.'
> Lewis Carroll, *Through The Looking Glass* (1872), Ch.5.

The next magic word that I'd like to talk to you about is 'breakthrough'.

People sometimes tell me that 'breakthrough' is a somewhat old-fashioned sounding word, and indeed it is. Advertisers and promoters have been using this word for centuries but, if you keep your eyes and ears open to current advertising material, you'll quickly find that 'breakthrough' is still as popular today as it was in your grandparents' time.

This is because it's an exciting word. It carries a sense of expectancy that something new has happened. It's also a greedy word, because it conveys a hidden message that you are among the first to hear about this development.

Put 'guarantee' and 'win' and 'breakthrough' together – the three magic words that I've introduced you to so far, and you can start creating sentences like:

It's a breakthrough! It's a winner! And what's more ... it's guaranteed!

Here's another:

I can guarantee that you'll be a winner with my breakthrough formula!

And another:

It's a breakthrough that guarantees you'll win every time!

SAVE TIME, NOT MONEY

The magic word that I'd now like to introduce you to is 'save'.

Now the interesting thing about 'save' is that I'm talking about saving you *time* as opposed to saving you *money*. That's because time is money nowadays. Tell your readers how much time your product or service can save them and they will listen to you with great interest. Tell them how much money you can save them and they may not listen to you with quite the same level of interest. That's because most people believe that they have already figured out the most cost-effective way to run their business or to buy goods and services.

But 'time' is a universally precious commodity and people are always interested in hearing about faster ways to do things or quicker ways to arrive at their destinations.

Not so very long ago, I received a wonderful sales letter in the post informing me that, if I used a certain form of public transport, the public authorities could 'guarantee' (there's that magic word again) that I would save an average of 30 minutes a day on my journey to and from my office. *'That's more than 2 hours a week'*, the message went on to tell me, *'which is 104 hours a year, which is more than a year saved in an average worker's life!'*. Put another way, by simply changing my method of transport to work, I could add an extra year's leisure time to my life!

That's not a bad offer by anybody's standards. It was certainly an offer that captured my attention because, in no time at all, I found myself with my calculator in hand and, very quickly, I established that it was true ... a savings of 30 minutes a day could actually add up to an extra year's free time for you to enjoy in your life.

Had they told me that I could save 10 cents off the cost of my journey, or 1 Euro a week, I don't believe that it would have made anything like the same impact on me.

Now, let's see if I can put together the four magic words that we've learned so far into one sentence. Here it is:

> Great news! With our **breakthrough** method of public transport, I **guarantee** you that you'll **save** so much time that you'll **win** a extra year's leisure time in your life.

Now, let me introduce a word of caution and assure you that, to capture attention, you don't have to use ALL the magic words in one sentence. The reason why, up to now, I have been creating sentences using all the magic words that I've introduced to you is because I want you to see for yourself how much fun you can have playing around with different permutations and combinations of these words.

It's an easy game to play and, with a bit of practice, you'll be surprised at how quickly you can master the art of using magic words in the opening sentences of your letters.

HOW TO ...

The next magic word that I'd like to tell you about is, in fact, two words ... 'how to'.

'How to ...' immediately followed by a benefit, or a promise of a benefit, is a sure-fire way of capturing your reader's attention.

'How to' can be used at the beginning of a sentence like:

◊   How to sell more.

◊   How to increase your turnover.

◊   How to improve your memory.

◊   How to win!

◊   How to make the breakthrough that you've always wanted.

Alternatively, 'how to' can be used in the main body of a sentence like:

◊   Let me show you **how to** win!

◊   Believe me, I know **how to** make you wealthy!

Do you get the idea? Every time I see the words 'how to' I think of a story I was told once about Dale Carnegie.

The story goes that, when Dale Carnegie wrote his extraordinary book, he presented it to a number of publishing houses to see whether they would be interested in publishing it. Initially, all he got was rejections: it seemed that nobody was interested in publishing his book. It was the wrong book, in the wrong place, at the wrong time in the history of America.

Then, one day, a publisher contacted Dale and said, in effect, *'I'll publish your book if you let me choose the title for it'*.

Dale agreed, and the rest is history!

Dale Carnegie's *How to Win Friends and Influence People* became one of the best selling books of all time. It sold millions of copies all over the world and, to this day, you can still buy it. In its heyday, it was the number two best-seller book in the world – beaten only to the number one slot by the *Bible*.

And when I think of the *Bible*, which is a good book, and Dale Carnegie's *How to Win Friends and Influence People*, which is what I would call a 'greedy book' (greedy for more friends and power), I always say to myself ... *'there you have it!'*.

There you have the unique combination that makes up all of us – goodness and greediness! There's goodness and greediness in everyone. If you can appeal to either of these motives, you will capture attention but, if you can appeal to both, you immediately double your chances of success.

In magic word-speak: This is your guaranteed way to win!

FREE, AT LAST!

I've only four more magic words to tell you about and my next little word is the word 'free'.

Free, Free, FREE ... you see it everywhere! But can I ask you to be very careful with your use of the word 'free'? You see, 'free' is the exception to all the other magic words that have gone before.

And the reason why 'free' is the exception is because – wait for it – nobody believes the word 'free'! It's the old, old saying: 'there's no such thing as a free lunch', and believe me there never is!

Picture this for a moment! You are driving home from work in the evening and there in front of you is a fabulous big billboard sign proudly announcing to everyone: 'FREE HAMBURGER!'

What's the first, the very first, nasty little sub-conscious thought that flickers into your mind when you read a sign saying: 'FREE HAMBURGER!'?

Well, if you're anything like me, the very first thought that comes to mind is 'how many hamburgers do I have to buy before I get my free hamburger?'.

That's the kind of nasty negative thoughts that the word 'free' creates in people's minds. Almost instantly, when you see the word 'free', your sub-conscious mind goes looking for the 'catch'. Deep down, you know in your heart that people don't normally give away things free. You know that there's a catch somewhere. Furthermore – and this is interesting – you are not happy until you discover what the catch is. So you keep on reading until you, in effect, prove to yourself that 'there's no such thing as a free hamburger'.

Professional copywriters know this. That's why, if I were writing the copy for this big FREE HAMBURGER billboard, I would take great care not to answer this *'what's the catch?'* question for you until the very end of my copy. This way, I will immediately increase my chances of getting you to read every word I write.

In my opinion, only an amateur would write the following: *'Free Hamburger with every six you buy!'*. You see, when you do this, you give away the entire story in the headline and many people won't read any further.

Whereas, if you head up your billboard advertisement with the words 'FREE HAMBURGER' and then go on to tell me how mouth-wateringly delicious these hamburgers are, so full of goodness and taste and so on and so forth, I still haven't discovered the answers to my all-important question: *'What's the catch?'* or, put another way, *'How many do I have to buy?'*.

In this situation, the chances are that I'll keep reading – and discovering all the wonderful things about your hamburgers – until, at last, I find the answer to my all-important question down there where the copywriter carefully positioned it – at the very bottom of the advertisement.

This way, by the time the question is answered to my satisfaction, I'll have learned just about everything that you want me to know about your hamburgers. Hmmmmmmm, I might just even be hungry enough to pull in and buy a few of your delicious hamburgers!

So please keep in mind that, while FREE is a very powerful magic word, a 'hidden-persuader', call it what you may, it's also a word that most people don't believe. The minute they see the word 'free', they'll read the copy looking for the 'catch'. And the good copywriter's job is to ensure that the reader reads everything before they are presented with the answer to the *'Where's the catch?'* question that is in their mind.

Now, if you play around with some of the magic words that we've discussed so far you'll come up with headlines and opening sentences to a letter like:

It's a breakthrough! It's a winner! It's guaranteed to save you time ... what's more it's FREE!

Winners can save time with our free breakthrough!

It's the guaranteed time-saving breakthrough for winners!

AT LAST ...

Your next magic word is really two words and they are: 'At Last!'. For example:

◊ At last, there is a better way!

◊ At last, the breakthrough that you have been waiting for is now here.

◊ At last, you can have what you want ... now!

◊ At last, it's free!

There is a wonderful vibrancy about these two words, 'at last', which never fails to make your reader sit up and pay attention. I use them all the time and it never ceases to amaze me how they can add an immediate sparkle to even the dullest of sentences.

Take, for example, a fairly commonplace sentence that reads: *'We believe that our products are the best available in the market'*.

Think how much more vibrant and interesting this sentence would be if it read:

At last! We believe that our products are the best available in the market.

When you read a sentence like this last one, you immediately want to know what happened? Why was your product not the best in the market before now? Did you do something new? Have you discovered a breakthrough? What's the winning formula? Why now?

All these unanswered questions that are racing through your mind can only be answered by 'reading on'! And this is exactly what you want your reader to do – **read on!**

Every time I look at the two magic words 'free' and 'at last!', somewhere in the back of my mind I always hear the voice of Martin Luther King Jr. echoing down the corridors of time in his inspired '*I have a dream*' speech:

'Free at last! Free at last! Thank God Almighty, we are free at last!'

Although he probably never even knew of the existence of the magic words, Martin Luther King captured two of them in this unforgettable closing sentence of his '*I have a dream*' speech ... 'free' ... 'at last!'.

ANOTHER 'NEW' WORD

Your next magic word is the word 'new'.

Here's another what I call 'goodness & greediness' word. Everybody likes to have **new** things. Furthermore, some people are willing to pay a premium price just so that they can be the first kid on the block with the newest, the latest and the most attention-grabbing item in the neighbourhood.

Think about it, the entire fashion industry is turbo-powered by new images, new styles, new colours, new seasonal looks and suchlike. And as quick as they come, they are gone ... '*What's new today is tomorrow's old*'.

Likewise, in the newspaper industry, there is a constant 24-hour pressure to come up with new news from all four corners of the compass, or 'breaking news' as it's more commonly called. Do you know the word 'NEWS' itself is derived from the four different cardinal points of the compass: **N** = North, **E** = East, **W** = West and **S** = South. **NEWS!**

Ask anybody in the motor industry when is the peak sales time of the year for new cars and invariably they will tell you that it's the beginning of a new year. So much so, that some of my clients in the motor industry tell me that, if sales are not up at the beginning of the year, they know that they will find it difficult, if not impossible, to meet their sales targets for the entire year. So the **new** sales figures at the start of a **new** year are vitally important to them.

There is a constant global demand for new ways of doing things, new ideas, new production processes and new inventions. All over the world, marketing experts are in never-ending competition with each other to create new award-winning campaigns and successful sales promotions.

Before you are even awake in the morning, copywriters like me are already busy at work on your subconscious mind while you are brushing your teeth. Chances are that, if you look at your tube of toothpaste, you'll discover the words 'New Formula' prominently displayed on the side of the tube, trying to capture your half-awake attention.

'New' is a powerful word, which in three simple letters can bring a considerable amount of added-value and impact to just about anything you write. For example, a marketing campaign can achieve an immediate uplift when it is presented as being a 'new campaign', a relatively straightforward product breakthrough can be hyped up no-end by calling it a 'new breakthrough', or a bargain can have a huge amount of perceived value immediately added to it by imaginatively describing it as a 'new bargain'.

Let's take the first sample sentence that I used at the end of the last section:

It's a breakthrough! It's a winner! It's guaranteed to save you time ... what's more it's FREE!

By simply changing the word 'free' to 'new', you instantly have a headline that is just, if not more, appealing:

It's a breakthrough! It's a winner! It's guaranteed to save you time ... what's more it's NEW!

Likewise, if you take the sentence:

Winners can save time with our free breakthrough!

And if you change the word 'free' to 'new', you end up with an equally interesting sentence:

Winners can save time with our **new** breakthrough!

Now, Now!

By now, it will probably come as no surprise to you to learn that your final magic word is the word 'Now'.

'Now' must be the ultimate greedy word. I want it! I want it free! I want it new. I want it guaranteed and **I WANT IT NOW!**

In the same way as few people will be satisfied with a promise of 'pie in the sky when you die' (even if it happens to be guaranteed by the World Bank!), many people get frustrated if, having made up their mind to go ahead and buy something, they discover that the particular item they want is not immediately available ... now!

That's why action-headlines and sentences such as: *'Call us now ...'*, *'Order now ...'*, *'Our telephone lines are now open ...'* are such powerful motivators. It's also the reason why the words *'Not now!'* can have such a strong de-motivating effect on most of us.

And there you have it!

Win ... Guarantee ... Breakthrough ... Save ... How to ... Free ... At Last ... New ... Now!

Now you know some of the most powerful 'magic words' in a professional copywriter's Sales Letter toolkit. Yes, of course, there are other magic words but these are among the most popular ones.

No doubt you will have your own favourite sales words and you may be disappointed to find that I haven't included them in my list. Just remember what's common to all the popular and proven magic words that I have given you above are two important things: without exception, each of these words is a 'goodness and greediness word'.

By this, I mean that they all offer you a promise, or a hint of a promise, that something good is about to happen which will satisfy some need, or greed, that is in you or your company.

If you want to add more words of your own to your toolkit of magic words, you should carefully check each one of them for a 'goodness and greediness' dimension. Remember, the words I have given you are the 'golden' words, the words that have been tried, proven and tested down all the years, all over the world and in many different languages ... **and they work!**

At this stage, you may be saying to yourself, in effect: *'Huh! So much for these magic words. They are all 'over-the-top' words which are probably perfect for copywriters and suchlike ... but I can't possibly use words like free ... at last ... breakthrough, etc ... in a sales letter for my company'.*

So let me respond to you by asking you this question: Are you sure? Are you absolutely sure that there isn't one, or even two words, in my list that you couldn't, with a wee bit of imagination, use? For example, how about the word: 'Now'?

◊ 'If you'd like to take advantage of this service now.'

◊ 'By attending to this matter now you may be able to etc etc.'

◊ 'Perhaps now is a good time for us to meet.'

Or, what about the word: 'Save'?

◊ 'It will save time if we discuss this matter in advance of our meeting.'

◊ 'To save you the trouble and expense of going to ..., etc.'

◊ 'This summary sheet will save you ..., etc.'

But even if you decide that the magic words are definitely not for you and your company, I still have some very good news for you. In fact, you could almost say I have kept the very best wine till the end.

The good news for you is this!

If I were to call the magic words that I have introduced to you so far 'golden words', there is still one word that I have yet to introduce to you. It's a word that is worth more than all the magic words combined.

It's a platinum word!

But before we go on, let's take a quick chapter break and summarise what we have covered so far.

SUMMARY OF CHAPTER 2:

HERE'S WHAT YOU SAY & HOW YOU SAY IT

☐ In addition to the magic words 'Win' and 'Guarantee', you now have seven more important magic words in your writer's toolkit: Breakthrough ... Save ... How to ... Free ... New ... Now ... At Last!

☐ Common to all the magic words is the fact that they are all 'greedy' words. They appeal to the human greediness that exists in most people. And this is probably the reason why they work so well at capturing readers' attention.

☐ The magic word 'free' is a word that has to be used with great care, because nowadays, most people are wary of anything that comes free, and they look for the 'catch'.

☐ In total, you now have nine magic words to use in your sales letters and, with a little imagination, you can use these words to create endless numbers of attention-capturing sentences.

☐ If we are to call these nine magic words the 'golden words', there is still one word − a word that is worth more than all the golden words combined − and this is the 'platinum' word that I will now introduce to you.

3. THE PLATINUM WORD IS 'YOU'

'Will you, won't you, will you, won't you, will you join the dance?'
Lewis Carroll, *Alice's Adventures in Wonderland* (1865), Ch.10.

The platinum word is 'You'. The more often you use the word 'You' in your sales letter, the more personal your communication is with your readers.

You are the most important person in the world. Everything about you is special. And when I talk about the word 'you', I mean every single possible variation of the word 'you' – for example: You; Your; You're; Yourself; Yourselves; Yours.

The moment you start using the word 'you' in your written communications and sales letters, something wonderful happens. Immediately, you are tapping in to 'you-me' communications. Immediately, you are 'talking' to your reader in a one-to-one style.

And this is one of the biggest secrets of success of how you write a very persuasive sales letter. Instead of 'we-us' correspondence, from the outset, you should always strive for a more personal 'you-me' communication style.

This is something that many large companies fail to do. All too often they tell you things like: *'We are the best! ... Contact us ... and we will supply the goods'*. How much nicer it would be if their message read: *'You are the best ... contact me ... and I will supply you with exactly what you require'*.

What we're talking about here is the power of 'you'. You see a really good sales letter – even though it may be sent to a very large audience or target group – should create, right from the beginning, the impression that it is being sent from one person to another person and it should get as far away as possible from the concept that it's simply a 'megaphone' message for a huge anonymous audience.

Get into the habit of using 'you' as often, and as early, in your letter as you can and you'll instinctively find yourself composing your letter with your reader's viewpoint in mind. This is a liberating exercise because, from the moment you start seeing things from your reader's viewpoint, you'll find yourself, almost automatically, explaining the benefits of your product or service to your reader's advantage. And this is exactly what your reader most wants to hear from you.

THE U-COUNT

Now let me tell you something very interesting, something that you can use to your immediate advantage. It's a little trick of the copywriter's trade and I call it the 'U-count'.

The 'U-count' is a very simple formula for enhancing your sales letter and here's how it works for you.

Every time you finish drafting your sales letters, count up the number of times the word 'you' – or any of the variations of the word you – your, yourself, etc. – appears in your draft, paying particular attention to your opening paragraph.

Quite simply, the more 'yous' you have in your letter, the better it is from an effective one-to-one communications viewpoint. If you find that you have no 'yous' at all in your draft, my advice to you is tear it up and start again. Because the chances are that you are not communicating with your reader. All you are doing is talking to yourself.

If your 'U-count' is very high, you have the makings of something very interesting in your hands – because a high 'U-count' means that you are very actively engaging your reader in a 'you-me' communications process. And this is the kind of communications process that your reader likes, and responds to, best.

If your 'U-count' is only so-so, you should go back and have another look at your draft letter and see whether there are any areas where you could possibly increase your 'U-count'.

Pay careful attention to your opening paragraph and try, wherever possible, to have a high 'U-count' in this very important paragraph. Better still; see whether you can introduce the word 'you' into your opening sentence.

Sometimes, it's a very useful exercise to print out a hard copy of your draft letter and use a yellow highlighter to carefully highlight for yourself every single ... you ... your ... you're ... yourself ... yourselves ... and ... yours ... on each page. This enables you to see at a glance whether the 'U-count' is distributed evenly on your page(s). What you are trying to avoid is the possibility of ending up with a 'curate's egg' of a 'U-count. (A 'curate's egg', for those of you who not familiar with the eating habits of those worthy people, is an egg that is good in some parts and bad in others.)

If you find that there is a feast of 'yous' in some parts of your letter, and a veritable famine of 'yous' in other parts of your letter, it's always worth your while to go back and have another look at those paragraphs, or areas in your letter, where your 'U-count' is low. See whether you can edit these areas slightly and increase your 'U-count' in those paragraphs.

Let me give you a quick example of what I mean. In the following letter, I've highlighted all the 'yous' that the letter contains. No paragraph has less than two 'yous' and some have a 'you' on just about every single line. What you see in this letter is not only a very high 'U-count' but also an excellent distribution of 'yous' throughout the letter as well.

Of course, the finished letter that was sent out in the mail to potential customers didn't have the 'yous' highlighted in yellow. I'm simply highlighting them here for you, so that you can immediately see what I mean when I talk about trying to achieve an even distribution of 'yous' throughout your letter.

P MANAHAN & CO Chartered Accountants
Carmichael House, 60 Baggot Street Lower, Dublin 2

Mr Robert Hayes-McCoy
Managing Director
Robert Hayes-McCoy Consultants Ltd
13 Lea Road
Sandymount
Dublin 4

Date

Dear Robert

Sometimes you're the windshield
Sometimes you're the bug ...
From the song, *The Bug*, by Dire Straits.

Do you ever get this feeling about your company's accountancy and financial planning workload? One moment you're on top of everything and the way forward is clear. Then wham! Something unexpected comes along and it messes up all your plans.

Welcome to the latest edition of *Solutions* newsletter. As you can see, we couldn't resist including the above line from the song, *The Bug*, on the back page of your newsletter.

Because we're coming up to the time of the year when many companies come under pressure to keep their accountancy workloads and forward-planning strategies moving forward. And we'd like you to know that we're available to give you a professional helping hand if you ever need to call on us.

Even if you have no immediate requirement for our services, you're very welcome to call me and ask me to come in for a **'no-obligation'** consultation discussion with you immediately. This way, I may be able to help you to identify some relatively self-contained tasks that you could very profitably delegate or sub-contract to us.

Perhaps we can assist you in drawing up your strategic development plan for the future. Or we might be able to give you valuable independent professional advice on some project that you've put on the long finger because you simply haven't **yet** found the time to give it the attention it deserves.

Whatever it is! Even if it's just for me to come in and have a general chat with you about the scope and the range of professional services that we can offer you, I'm looking forward to receiving your call. My telephone number is **01 123 4567** and you're very welcome to call me now while you have our latest edition of *Solutions* in your hands.

Yours sincerely

Peter V. Manahan
Managing Partner

Remember, the greater your 'U-count', the more you are engaging in 'you-me' communication with your reader. And the more consistent your high 'U-count' is from the start to the finish of your letter, the more consistently you engage your reader in one-to-one communication – and, therefore, the more difficult it is for your reader not to read all of your letter.

A uniformly high 'U-count' not only makes your sales letter more interesting to read, but it also makes it very hard for your reader not to read every word that you write to him or her.

SUMMARY OF CHAPTER 3:
HERE'S WHAT YOU SAY AND HOW YOU SAY IT

☐ The Platinum word is the word 'You'.

☐ This encompasses all the variations of the word 'You': Your ... You're ... Yourself ... Yourselves ... Yours.

☐ The more often you use the platinum word in your sales letter, the more personal your communication is with your readers.

☐ The 'U-count' is a very useful formula for you to use to establish how high the level of personal communication is in your sales letters.

☐ A really good sales letter should have a consistently high 'U-count' in every paragraph so, before you sign off on your final draft, it's worth your while to check that you have achieved an even distribution of 'yous' throughout your letter.

4. A Word of Caution about Magic Words

> 'That's the reason they're called lessons,' the Gryphon remarked, 'because they lessen from day to day'.
> Lewis Carroll, *Alice's Adventures in Wonderland* (1865), Ch.9.

Have a look at this gravestone that I came across one day in a pet's cemetery in the gardens of a large stately mansion.

Have you noticed anything interesting about this gravestone? Have you spotted how poor Tommy was a widower for 10 years? His wife, Magic, died in 1926, while Tommy lived on to 1936. Yes! Magic died young!

There's a very important strategy message here that I want you to keep in mind when you are writing your sales letters. Never forget that ...

MAGIC DIES YOUNG!

Magic dies young! Once you've captured my attention with a magic word (or two) in your opening paragraph, your next job is to hold on to my attention for as long as you possibly can.

And the best way for you to do this is to make me settle down and become interested in finding out more about your proposition. Keep in mind that the reason why direct marketing copywriters like to use the magic words in the opening paragraphs and headlines of our sales letters and promotional material is to make the copy jump off the page and capture your attention ... to give it wings, as it were, and to get everything off to a flying start.

Once you've done this, you have achieved your purpose and what you must now do is to make me **settle down** and pay attention to the details of your proposition. If you keep on using magic words in the rest of your sales letter, the result will be that you'll have me over-hyped with greedy motivators and I'll find it very hard to come down to earth to a practical decision-making mode.

Furthermore, if you keep on using magic words, there is a very real danger that your copy may end up sounding downright silly. Here's an example of how an overuse of the magic words can result in somewhat trite, silly, unbelievable copy.

Dear Sir / Madam

At last, the opportunity you have been waiting for is here. **Now,** for the first time ever, we have added formula X to product Y and come up with a **breakthrough new** solution that will allow you to **save** both time and money.

Not only is this a **new breakthrough** but it's **guaranteed.** Furthermore, if you buy it **now** you will **win** the admiration and respect of both your bosses and peers. And it's even better than this.

Because when I tell you **how to** use it to its maximum potential, you will quickly realise that **now, at last**, you are **free**.

And the good news is that, if you place your order with us immediately, you are entitled to a **breakthrough** discount of 50% off the normal purchase price. This discount is **guaranteed**. So, **at last**, you have an exciting **new** offer that is a real **win**ner. It's available **now**!

An example of how an overuse of the magic words can result in somewhat trite, silly, unbelievable copy.

It's absolutely corny, isn't it? There's too much sales hype. This is what happens when you keep on using the magic words throughout your sales letter … you are constantly hyping up your readers with sales babble and you are not giving them enough 'mental time' to settle down and concentrate on your offer.

To get maximum value from the magic words, therefore, you must use them sparingly and carefully. My advice to you is to definitely use one – perhaps two – magic words in your opening paragraph and then ease off using them, because the positive effects of their 'magic dies young!'.

But, whatever you do, don't ever stop using the platinum word 'You'.

Start with the magic! Then aim to have a consistently high 'U-count' all throughout your letter, and you are well on your way to writing a very persuasive sales letter.

SUMMARY OF CHAPTER 4:
HERE'S WHAT YOU SAY AND HOW YOU SAY IT

☐ Now that you know the magic words and have seen how they work, it's time to introduce a word of caution.

☐ Magic dies young!

☐ If you overuse the magic words in your sales letter, there is a very real danger that your letter will sound 'over the top' and you will effectively kill your entire sales message.

☐ Within reason, however, it's safe to say that you can never overuse the platinum word 'You'.

☐ So the ideal approach for you to take with your sales letters is to use a magic word, or two, in your opening paragraph to immediately capture your readers' attention and then settle down and hold on to your readers' interest by using a consistently high 'U-count' in all of the following paragraphs.

5. THE 'LADY IN RED'

> 'Contrariwise,' continued Tweedledee, 'if it was so, it might be; and if it were so, it would be, but as it isn't, it ain't. That's logic.'
> Lewis Carroll, *Through The Looking Glass* (1872), Ch.4.

Now is the time for me to introduce you to a little stratagem of the copywriter's trade – a tactic that I often use to get started with my own sales letters. It's a useful little formula, which is not only challenging and stimulating to use, but it can give you some fabulous opening lines and paragraphs for your letters. It also has a certain logic about it that I find very appealing.

You see, sometimes – in fact, if I'm to be honest with you, most times – when I sit down to start writing a sales letter, my mind goes absolutely blank.

It's at times like this when I'm tempted to go and get myself a cup of coffee or pick up the phone and make a telephone call or do anything, anything at all, to fill that dreadful void in my mind.

These are frustrating times for anyone who has a sales letter to write, especially if you are working to a tight time deadline. Because if you are not careful, you may end up several hours, and many cups of coffee, later with an absolutely blank sheet of paper still in front of you. What we're talking about here is the universal writers' curse of 'getting started'.

Don't ever let this happen to you. What you must do is look out the window, or close your eyes, and quickly write down the very first sentence that comes into your head. It doesn't matter what the sentence is – just write it down!

It could be something like *'Today is a nice day'*. Alternatively, it might be something along the lines of *'The traffic was very heavy coming into work this morning'*, or *'I forgot to feed the dog'*. Whatever it is that first comes into your mind, write it down immediately.

Right now, as I'm sitting here writing this paragraph, an absolutely stunning-looking lady dressed in a red T-shirt has passed my window. So, to give you a practical example of what I want you to do, I'm going to write down the following sentence on a sheet of paper: *'The lady in red looks fabulous'*.

THE *'LADY IN RED'* LOOKS FABULOUS

So far, so good, now I've started. The next thing I must do is check the sentence that I've written down and see if it contains an all-important magic word. If it does, I'm happy, because I can move immediately on to the next stage.

If it doesn't contain a magic word, what I must do is see whether I can pop one into the sentence somewhere. As you can see, my sentence *'The lady in red looks fabulous'* doesn't contain any magic words. So I've got to ask myself where I can fit one in? In this case, the very first magic word that comes into my mind is the word 'now'. So I'm going to add this into my sentence as follows:

The lady in red **now** looks fabulous.

Now, I've got my sentence with my magic word and it's time for me to move on to the next stage. This is the stage where the real creativity begins. Because the letter that I have to work on today is a promotional letter for a bank. They have asked me to write a letter that they can send out to customers who have an 'unofficial' overdraft. They want to tell these customers that unofficial overdrafts are not permitted and they wish to invite every customer who has an unofficial overdraft to come in at once and talk to their bank manager about taking out a Term Loan, which will immediately pay off their unapproved overdraft and get their finances in order, as it were. Uh Oh! Tough one, this.

And it's not going to be made any easier when you see what I plan to do with my *'Lady in Red'* sentence. What I'm going to do is make this totally oddball sentence the opening sentence of my letter to every customer of the bank who has an unofficial overdraft.

Hey! Stop! Wait a minute! I can't do that. I can't just write down the very first sentence that comes into my mind and use it as the first sentence in an important letter like this.

You bet I can! Here's how my letter unfolds:

Dear Mr Hayes-McCoy

The lady in red now looks fabulous!

Since the beginning of this year, her bank account was constantly in the red but, now that she's met her bank manager, she's never looked back because her account is always in the black.

By converting her overdraft into a Term Loan, not only is she is able to manage her account more efficiently, but she's saving a considerable amount of money on her interest payments too! All it took was one quick meeting with her bank manager and she ... .

This is not bad at all! I've got an attention-capturing opening sentence that includes a magic word. I've managed to use creativity to link up the lady in red to the overdraft situation that the bank wants me to write about. In fact, I'm quite proud of myself. And if it wasn't for the fact that there are two little 'niggles' at the back of my mind, all I have to do now is finish off this letter and I'm laughing all the way to the bank.

Problem is, and this is my first little niggle; I know that no bank in its right mind will accept this letter from me. It's a good letter. In fact, it's great, but it's just not what the client wants.

And my next little niggle is that it's got an absolutely zero 'U-count'. Not one of those 93 words that I've written above is a 'you', which all goes to prove that I am totally indulging myself by showing you how creatively clever I am at writing myself out of tight corners and that what I've just written, if you'll pardon the pun, 'is for the birds!'.

Actually, this is not true. What I've just done is something very useful and practical. In no time at all, I'll have the makings of a great sales letter in my hands – a letter that my client, the bank, will be happy to pay me for without any quibbles whatsoever, because it will successfully sell the idea to their customers that an authorised Term Loan is a more effective and acceptable way of managing their money than an unofficial overdraft.

Because what I'm now going to do is put down my pen and pick up my editing scalpel. I'm going to ruthlessly cut out all the bits that won't work, are not acceptable, are not needed, and I'm going to see what happens. The rule of using the ruthless editing scalpel is ... **Always, always start with the first paragraph.**

By this I mean, totally cut out the first paragraph and see whether your letter still makes sense without it. In this case, the first paragraph is a single sentence: *'The lady in red now looks fabulous'*. So let's cut this out entirely.

Let's see how the opening paragraph of the cut-down version of my letter now reads?

Hey! It's not bad ...

Dear Mr Hayes-McCoy

Since the beginning of this year, her bank account was constantly in the red but, now that she's met her bank manager, she's never looked back because her account is always in the black.

It's certainly an interesting opening for a letter. But okay, let's face it; it's not going to work in this case because, since I've cut out the original *'Lady in Red'* opening paragraph this second paragraph, which refers to *'her'* and *'she'* meeting her bank manager won't make any sense at all to the reader.

So apply the ruthless editing scalping rule again: zap this 'new' first paragraph as well. At this stage, I've completely cut out paragraphs 1 and 2 and what I'm now left with is my original third paragraph. Let's have a look at how the opening paragraph of my drastically cut-down letter now reads:

Dear Mr Hayes-McCoy

By converting her overdraft into a Term Loan, not only is she is able to manage her account more efficiently, but she's saving a considerable amount of money on her interest payments too! All it took was one quick meeting with her bank manager and she ... .

Believe it or not, now I'm getting places! I really am.

What I now need to do is a further little bit of editing and to increase my 'U-count'. You see, as it now stands, this opening paragraph is talking about a third person. See what happens when I edit it ever so slightly and talk to the reader in a me-you format.

Dear Mr Hayes-McCoy

Do you know that, by converting your overdraft into a Term Loan, not only will you be able to manage your account more efficiently, but you'll save a considerable amount of money on your interest payments too!

All it takes is one quick meeting with your bank manager and you ...

Done it! Now I've got the beginning of a 'real' letter on my hands – a letter that works, a letter that has the magic word 'save' in the opening sentence, a high 'U-count' and, above all, a letter that's beginning to sound interesting!

But what happened to my *'Lady in red'*? Actually she's gone! Gone forever! She's done her job. I don't need her any more so, as you can see, my ruthless editing scalpel has cut her entirely out of my letter.

Now let's just pause for a moment and find out why did I bother using the *'Lady in red'* in the first place? What use was she to me? You could even say that she was no use to me at all. In fact, she probably made everything just a little bit harder for me. Because she forced me to think and re-think and think again as I tried to work my way forward towards creating the beginning of a 'real' letter – a letter that my client could use.

Read that sentence again: ... **She forced me to think and re-think and think again as I tried to work my way forward** ...

There you have your answer! Effectively the *'Lady in red'* is a 'stalking-horse', which is a horse used as a decoy as you steal unnoticed up to your prey or your target. In my case, what I was trying to capture was a good opening sentence for my letter. But my creative mind was a blank, it just wouldn't co-operate. It was going all over the place on me.

And I know from experience that, when my mind becomes stubborn and unhelpful like this, I'm wasting my time trying to force it to co-operate with me. So I have to approach the problem with stealth. That's where my *'Lady in red'* stalking-horse comes in. Because the moment I signal to my mind that this is my first sentence and, come what may, I am not going to change it, my creative mind goes into overdrive and concentrates immediately on the question *'What am I going to say next?'*.

Believe me, *'What am I going to say next?'* is a far, far easier and more focused question for a letter-writer, who is faced with a blank sheet of paper, to answer than it is for him or her to answer a totally open-ended question like: *'But how will I start?'*.

Try this 'stalking horse' approach for yourself next time you have an important sales letter to write. I think you'll be pleasantly surprised at how constructively creative your mind can be when your force it to focus in on answering *'What will I say next?'*.

To get your sales letter off to a flying start, just write down the first sentence that comes into your mind and please don't try to 'mentally' edit this sentence in advance. No matter how zany, off-the-wall or indeed downright uninteresting your sentence is, just write it down exactly as it comes into your head.

THE STALKING-HORSE FORMULA

In the sample *'Lady in red'* opening sentence that I used above, my mind jumped out the window and acknowledged the good-looking lady that just walked past. I could have approached this opening sentence challenge in any number of more conventional and straightforward ways such as:

Dear Sir

We beg to refer to your overdrawn bank account ...

Dear Sir

We wish to advise you that your bank account is overdrawn and ...

Dear Sir

We regret to inform you that the current overdrawn position of your bank account is not acceptable ...

Dear Sir

We would like to meet you to discuss your unacceptable overdrawn account ...

There is absolutely no end to the number of different ways I could have opened my letter. And while all of the above openings can – and often are – used to begin a letter such as this, they are not, in my opinion, as good as the opening that the *'Lady in red'* has helped me to create.

The opening that the *'Lady in red'* eventually led me to is superior, because it captures your attention and makes you want to read on in an open and positive frame of mind:

> Do you know that, by converting your overdraft into a Term Loan, not only will you be able to manage your account more efficiently. but you'll save a considerable amount of money on your interest payments too!

This stalking-horse formula, whereby I start drafting my letter by simply writing down the very first sentence that comes into my mind, is not only one that I have been successfully using for years but it's also great fun.

The fun element comes from the fact that you have absolutely no idea where it's going to lead you. It's a challenging invigorating formula that puts you on the fast lane to creative thinking and creative writing from the outset.

Furthermore, and this is important, eight times out of 10, you'll find that if you can get off to a strong creative start, everything else in your letter falls quickly and simply into place for you. As the old saying goes, *'well begun is the job half done'*.

Keep this in mind next time you 'pick up the pen' to write a sales letter and try – try hard – to avoid doing what so many letter writers do, which is to write the first paragraph by rote. Writing by rote inevitably leads to openings such as

> Dear Sir
>
> I beg to refer to yours of the 16th ultimo ...

> Dear Sir
>
> We wish to draw your attention to the fact that ...

> Dear Sir
>
> Further to our previous correspondence about this matter ...

Dear Sir

I refer to previous communications ...

The reason why so many people open their letters in a 'writing by rote' mode is because, quite simply, they are not paying enough attention to what they are actually writing in the current paragraph. Instead, they are thinking ahead to what they are going to say in their next paragraph. From a professional copywriter's viewpoint this is a very dangerous – sometimes fatal – thing to do. Because, inevitably, the results will be that your opening paragraph will be lack-lustre, boring, tired and, possibly, even trite. Because the opening paragraph is far and away the most important paragraph in your entire letter, this is exactly what you cannot afford to let happen.

David Ogilvy, the founder of Ogilvy and Mather, one of the world's greatest direct marketing agencies, tells how he gathered all his copywriters into a room and said:

Ladies and gentlemen, when you have written the headline, you have spent 75% of your client's money.

By this he meant that, unless the headline in your brochure, or the opening paragraph of your direct mail letter, has the power to hold your readers' attention, three out of every four of them will not read any further. Wow! Imagine losing 75% of your readers' attention just because you start your letter with a weak or uninteresting headline or opening paragraph.

That's why you have to work very hard to make absolutely certain that your opening paragraph or your headline is a good one. So take your time with it. Get this fundamental right and your draft sales letter will be well on its way to becoming a very persuasive sales letter. Get it wrong and you effectively kill your reader's interest before you start.

And do you know something! If you get it wrong, you'll find that you are also killing your own enthusiasm and interest in your letter as well. There is nothing that gives me more dissatisfaction that trying to finish a sales letter that I know has got off to a bad start.

SUMMARY OF CHAPTER 5:
HERE'S WHAT YOU SAY AND HOW YOU SAY IT

☐ The opening paragraph of any sales letter is far and away the most important paragraph of the entire letter. You see, just about everybody is prepared to invest time in reading the opening paragraph but, if the opening paragraph is not strong enough to hold their attention, as many as three out of every four of your readers will read no further.

☐ That's why you must take great care to get your opening paragraph right. This takes time. Be prepared to invest the time in it.

☐ One useful way of overcoming writers' block is to use the 'stalking-horse' formula to create the first sentence of your sales letter.

☐ This involves writing down the very first thing that comes into your mind and then playing a game with yourself to see how effectively you can link what you have written down on paper to the real subject matter of your sales letter.

☐ This tactical approach often creates very interesting and dynamic opening paragraphs for your sales letters, especially if you can manage to include a magic word in your first sentence.

6. Getting It Right by Editing from the Top

> 'You know', he said very gravely, 'it's one of the most serious things that can possibly happen to one in a battle – to get one's head cut off'.
> Lewis Carroll, *Through the Looking Glass* (1865), Ch.4.

In my last chapter, I introduced you to the 'stalking-horse' strategy as an interesting and useful way of getting started with your sales letter. An important part of this strategy involves 'editing from the top', which inevitably – but not always – means that your stalking-horse disappears once its job is done.

Remember, you don't always have to use 'the stalking-horse' strategy to begin your sales letters; it's just a useful little 'kick-start' tactic to have up your sleeve, if you are ever facing a blank sheet of paper and writer's block sets in. Also, it's an interesting way of coming up with unusual, attention-capturing, opening paragraphs.

Many writers have a pretty good idea of what they want to say in their sales letters and don't need to play around with ladies in red and suchlike to get started. But no matter what way you start, and no matter how pleased you are with the way your draft letter is shaping up for you, it's always wise to apply the 'edit from the top' formula to it before you finally sign off on your sales letter. Because 'editing from the top' can also help you to:

◊   Cut out unwanted paragraphs

◊   Reduce the size of an overlong letter

◊   Rearrange the order of your paragraphs so as to achieve maximum impact and efficiency.

Cutting out unwanted paragraphs and rearranging the order of things in your letter is part of the editing process. And, sometimes, a simple little bit of paragraph rearranging can turn a mediocre sales letter into a very persuasive sales letter with a few quick strokes of the pen.

Let me give you an example of how this works.

> Dear Mr Goldpenny
>
> My grandmother swore by it! My mother used one every single day of her married life. Often, my father used to say that our home just wouldn't be the same without it. And, of course, now that I'm married with children of my own, I have to say that I agree with him.
>
> It makes everyone feel so warm and cosy, especially on cold winter nights when you can hear the wind howling outside. It brings such rich comfort and a wonderful sense of security to the house that I can't ever imagine what my life would be without one.
>
> If you're lucky enough to have a beautiful cast-iron **Robertino** solid fuel cooker in your kitchen, I think you'll agree with me when I say that this must be the best investment you can ever make in your home.
>
> And, if you were one of the wise ones who paid the extra €150 for the luxury top of the range TR/24 model, you must be absolutely delighted with all the additional benefits and savings you ...

This is a nice letter! You can see what the copywriter is up to. He's gently teasing you at the beginning of the letter by slowly – ever so slowly – building up an atmosphere of warm family comforts. Until you reach the third paragraph, you have no idea what this letter is about or where it is going.

Then you read that wonderful sentence:

> If you're lucky enough to have a beautiful cast iron **Robertino** solid fuel cooker in your kitchen, I think you'll agree with me when I say that this must be the best investment you can ever make in your home.

The interesting thing about this letter, and the reason why I am using it as an example for you here, is that if you apply the 'edit from the top' strategy to it and cover up the first paragraph, you'll find that it still works as a teaser opening.

Yes, indeed! You could actually start this letter on the second paragraph.

> It makes everyone feel so warm and cosy, especially on cold winter nights when you can hear the wind howling outside. It brings such rich comfort and a wonderful sense of security to the house that I can't ever imagine what my life would be without one.

Now, let's cover up the second paragraph as well and see if the letter still makes sense.

> Dear Mr Goldpenny
>
> My grandmother swore by it! My mother used one every single day of her married life. Often, my father used to say that our home just wouldn't be the same without it. And, of course, now that I'm married with children of my own, I have to say that I agree with him.
>
> It makes everyone feel so warm and cosy, especially on cold winter nights when you can hear the wind howling outside. It brings such rich comfort and a wonderful sense of security to the house that I can't ever imagine what my life would be without one.
>
> If you're lucky enough to have a beautiful cast-iron **Robertino** solid fuel cooker in your kitchen, I think you'll agree with me when I say that this must be the best investment you can ever make in your home.

And it does! In fact, there is no question about it, this third paragraph is the real jewel in the crown, because not only does your message still make sense when you use this as the opening paragraph of your sales letter, but you are drawing your reader in much quicker, and far more effectively, to the core benefits of your product:

> If you're lucky enough to have a beautiful cast iron **Robertino** solid fuel cooker in your kitchen ...

Make no mistake about it; this is the opening paragraph that you are looking for – a sentence that contains no less than six uses of the platinum magic word 'You'.

But, in the interest of completing the exercise, don't give up on the 'edit from the top' strategy for the moment. Try covering up this third paragraph as well, and see how your letter reads.

Dear Mr Goldpenny

And if you were one of the wise ones who paid the extra €150 for the luxury top of the range TR/24 model. you must be absolutely delighted with all the additional benefits and savings you ...

It's not going to work, is it?

That's because an opening like this won't make any sense to your readers. And even if you tidy it up by leaving out the first word 'And', so that your opening sentence now reads ... *'If you were one of the wise ones ...'*, it still wouldn't make sense. You've reached the point where the 'edit from the top' system tells you to go back to the previous paragraph, where everything still makes sense, and use this as your opening paragraph. It's almost as if a divine hand is directing you back to the best opening paragraph of all for your letter.

But what are we going to do with the original two warm and delightfully atmospherically-charged opening paragraphs? Are we going to discard them completely? You see, I particularly like the first one: *'My grandmother swore by it!'*. The reason I like it so much is because everything about this paragraph is a wonderful homely testimonial for the **Robertino** solid fuel cooker.

So while I've made the decision not to use it as my opening paragraph, let's see what happens if I insert it immediately after my new opening paragraph. If I do this, my newly-structured letter is now going to read like this:

Dear Mr Goldpenny

If you're lucky enough to have a beautiful cast-iron **Robertino** solid fuel cooker in your kitchen, I think you'll agree with me when I say that this must be the best investment you can ever make in your home.

My grandmother swore by it! My mother used one every single day of her married life. Often, my father used to say that our home just wouldn't be the same without it. And, of course, now that I'm married with children of my own, I have to say that I agree with him.

And if you were one of the wise ones who paid the extra €150 for the luxury top of the range TR/24 model, you must be absolutely delighted with all the additional benefits and savings you ...

Now, after a little bit of paragraph rearrangement, I've definitely got the makings of a very interesting sales letter in my hands:

◊ A sales letter that opens with a strong attention-grabbing paragraph which focuses in on the product being sold

◊ And which is immediately followed up with a very interesting 'testimonial'-style paragraph, which tells you that my grandmother, my mother, my father and myself all agree that the **Robertino** solid fuel cooker must be one of the best investments that you can ever make in your home. It's as if my entire family are giving you a personal guarantee of satisfaction.

The practical lesson to be learned here is that, when you are editing from the top to establish whether you have the strongest possible opening paragraph for your sales letter, you don't have to discard everything that goes before a paragraph that you might finally decide to use as your new opening paragraph.

In the sample exercise, that I've just completed for you, I simply promoted my original paragraph 3 up into opening paragraph position. Then I demoted my original opening paragraph into the paragraph 2 slot and I eliminated my original second paragraph entirely. And it works!

HERE'S A LITTLE FUN GAME

Have a look at letters A & B below and see whether you can pick out correctly the opening paragraph and subsequent paragraph rearrangements that I decided to use in the final draft of my letter after I applied the 'edit from the top' formula.

Letter A:

Original Draft	Final Draft
Dear Mr Goldpenny	Dear Mr Goldpenny
We're asking our key business associates to support us by taking out an advert in this Special Newspaper Report.	**We're asking our key business associates to support us by taking out an advert in this Special Newspaper Report.**
Since just about everybody has a parent or an elderly relative that, at some stage in their lives, could benefit from nursing care facilities all the indications are that this Report will become a valuable reference document in many households.	On Friday 27th June 200X, the prime minister has been invited to perform the official opening in Sweetmount of St. Anne's Nursing Home for the Elderly. The ceremony also marks the public launch of one of the largest Healthcare Groups in the country – **ABC Healthcare**.
It's a report that will give guidance and advise to everybody who is interested in knowing about nursing home facilities for the elderly in Ireland.	To mark the occasion we have commissioned **The National Herald** to write a special report on Saturday 5th July 200X about 'Caring for The Elderly'.
It will contain information about the tax relief available to family members who are contributing towards the cost of a parent's stay in a nursing home, plus a wealth of other very useful financial and family budgeting information.	Since just about everybody has a parent or an elderly relative that, at some stage in their lives, could benefit from nursing care facilities all the indications are that this Report will become a valuable reference document in many households.
On Friday 27th June 200X, the prime minister has been invited to perform the official opening in Sweetmount of St. Anne's Nursing Home for the Elderly. The ceremony also marks the public launch of one of the largest Healthcare Groups in the country – **ABC Healthcare**.	It's a report that will give guidance and advise to everybody who is interested in knowing about nursing home facilities for the elderly in Ireland.
To mark the occasion we have commissioned **The National Herald** to write a special report on Saturday 5th July 200X about 'Caring for The Elderly'.	It will contain information about the tax relief available to family members who are contributing towards the cost of a parent's stay in a nursing home, plus a wealth of other very useful financial and family budgeting information.
And so on ...	And so on ...

In letter A, my own 'edit from the top' exercise quickly identified the last two paragraphs as being the strongest and most impactful paragraphs to use as the opening paragraphs of the letter. By simply moving these two paragraphs into the first and second paragraph slots, I created what I believe is a more effective sales letter.

Letter B:

Original Draft	Final Draft
Dear Mr Goldpenny **It's Mid-Summer Party Time ...** **And You Are Invited** The party is happening at ABC Car Dealers on Mid-Summer's weekend, Saturday 21st and Sunday 22nd June, and we're really looking forward to you and your family joining us for the celebrations. **It's going to be fun**! All our cars are looking forward to it, and you wouldn't believe how many of them are lined up for the party festivities. It's our biggest selection ever! Even if you are not thinking of buying, our cars are hoping you'll come along and have a little spin in the model you fancy. Because, believe me, there are some very elegant models all lined up to capture your attention. And every single car is hoping that you'll have a little test drive in them so that they can show off to you how good they are and what superb value they are for money too! Now, you've heard of Hen Parties and Stag Parties but I bet you've never heard of a **MID-SUMMER CAR PARTY!** And so on ...	Dear Mr Goldpenny **It's Mid-Summer Party Time ...** **And You Are Invited** You've heard of Hen Parties and Stag Parties but I bet you've never heard of a **MID-SUMMER CAR PARTY!** That's what's happening at ABC Car Dealers on Mid-Summer's weekend, Saturday 21st and Sunday 22nd June, and we're really looking forward to you and your family joining us for the celebrations. **Because it's going to be fun**! All our cars are looking forward to it too, and you wouldn't believe how many of them are lined up for the party festivities. It's our biggest selection ever! And every single car is hoping that you'll come along and have a little test drive in them so that they can show off to you how good they are and what superb value they are for money too! Even if you are not thinking of buying, our cars are hoping you'll come along and have a little spin in the model you fancy. Because, believe me, there are some very elegant models all lined up to capture your attention. And so on ...

In Letter B, my 'edit from the top' exercise quickly identified the last paragraph as being the best one to open this letter, so I moved it to the top and, with a few small changes to the copy and a little bit of rearranging of the paragraphs 4 and 5, everything fell very nicely into place.

SUMMARY OF CHAPTER 6:
HERE'S WHAT YOU SAY AND HOW YOU SAY IT

- ☐ No matter how happy you are with it, when you finish your draft letter it's always useful to go back and 'edit from the top' to see whether there is a more powerful opening paragraph available to you further down in your draft letter. If there is, use it!

- ☐ However, if you decide to use a 'later' paragraph of your draft letter as the opening paragraph in your finished letter, this doesn't mean that you have to discard all the earlier paragraphs of your draft letter. You may find that you still want to hold on to one or more if them in your newly structured letter and this is Okay!

- ☐ In fact, this is one of the very useful things about editing from the top because, not only does it help you to strengthen your opening paragraph, but it can help you also to rearrange paragraphs in a logical and interesting way, resulting in a much stronger sales letter.

7. A Good Testimonial is a Guarantee

'They told me you had been to her,
And mentioned me to him,
She gave me a good character
But said I could not swim.'
Lewis Carroll, *Alice's Adventures in Wonderland* (1865), Ch.10.

Because good testimonials can play such an important part in the successful promotion of your products or services in your sales letters, in this chapter I'd like to show you how you can get good testimonials – the best!

Because, properly used, testimonials can be worth their weight in gold. For example, if a bank, a well-known personality or a large respected company is prepared to give your product or service a testimonial, effectively they are endorsing it with an implied guarantee.

Never underestimate the sales power of a good testimonial. Problem is, most companies just don't know how to get good testimonials. Yes! In all my years of experience of looking at company brochures and promotional material, I have long ago come to the conclusion that most testimonials used by companies are – for want of a better word – 'blancmange'.

My reason for calling them by this name is because blancmange is pale, tasteless, unmemorable and decidedly wobbly!

In my experience, far too many testimonials that proudly feature on company brochures and websites are too long! They waffle. They use cumbersome words. Worst still, they lack impact. So much so that, chances are, if you ask somebody five minutes after they have read it to tell you what exactly the testimonial said, they won't remember.

I often use this little memory test with randomly-selected promotional material in my seminars and workshops and it never ceases to amaze me how quickly 'forgettable' so many testimonials are. This is either because the testimonials that are used to support the promotional message don't say anything very memorable in the first place, or else they are so long that, by the time you get to the end of reading them, your mind is suffering from mental-overload.

I believe that there is a very simple reason why so many business organisations are forced to rely on 'blancmange' testimonials to endorse their products and services. It's because they didn't ask for them properly in the first place.

You see, if you ask a customer or a supplier to give you a testimonial, the moment they agree to do this for you, they have burdened themselves with a difficult job. Because they are now faced with the question of *'What am I going to say?'*. And this is a far harder task than you might think. Often, they are afraid that, if they go over-the-top in their praise of your products or services, they may end up looking a bit foolish. They might even fear that, if they say something really positive, like *'Simply the best I have ever experienced!'*, people may scorn their ignorance or, worse still, you might be tempted to increase the price of your service to them. After all, you may reason, if your service to them is as good as they say it is in their testimonial, maybe they'll be prepared to pay more for it.

What many people do, when faced with the unenviable task of supplying a testimonial to a friend or supplier, is to take the easy way out. They write overlong bland sentences – sentences that lack any real bite. Somewhat like blancmange!

So let me ask you a question. And my question to you is this: *'How do you get a good testimonial for your company, product or service – the best?'*.

The answer is simple! You write your own testimonials.

Hey! Stop! Steady on there! Before you think that you are in the hands of a crook who is telling you to lie through your teeth and write your own testimonials, can I quickly assure you that you are in safe honest hands. When I advise you to write your own testimonials, what I mean is sit yourself down and grab a sheet of paper and write down a half a dozen or so good, true, complimentary things that you would like other people to say about your products or services.

Then pick up your telephone and call your bank manager, best customers, leading personality in your locality, or whoever it is that you have in mind to give you a testimonial. And, in the course of asking them whether they would give you the favour of a testimonial, tell them up-front that you have written down a couple of sample testimonials on a sheet of paper. Explain to them that what you would like them to do is have a look at your list of testimonials and, perhaps, put their name beside the one that appeals to them most!

Simple isn't it! And do you know what? It works! In the vast majority of cases, you'll find that your clients and best customers will be quite happy to put their name beside one of the sample testimonials that you have given them.

What often happens when you present a client with a list to choose from is that they will tell you that they are happy to put their name beside a number of different supplied testimonials and that they will willingly fit in with your preferences as to which one you would best like them to endorse.

Sometimes, and I've seen this happen, a client will tell you that they don't like anything on your supplied list and that they would rather write their own testimonial. Believe it or not, this is good news! Because when this happens, in nine cases out of 10, you'll find that they will actively use your supplied list as a template for what they will put in their own testimonial. So, if your supplied list contains a selection of short snappy sound-bites, which effectively makes the best testimonial of all, they, in turn, will feel obliged to come back to you with a similar kind of short, snappy and very complimentary 'sound-bite' testimonial.

A strong testimonial, introduced to your readers with the use of the magic word 'guarantee', gives you the best of all worlds. Because it allows you to say positive things in your sales letter like:

'As you can see from the enclosed testimonials, our products are proven and tested in the marketplace and are **guaranteed** to give you complete satisfaction.'

A strong, clear call-to-action testimonial can add a wonderfully positive 'tone' to your sales letters, which, in turn, will help you to achieve the higher level of sales breakthrough that you desire.

Far and away the most effective positioning of a testimonial in your sales letter is in the second or third paragraph. But, sometimes, a testimonial can be so strong, and promise such an attractive benefit to your readers, that it may deserve pride of place in the very first paragraph of your sales letter.

In fact, I'll go even further than this and say that a very strong, or unusual, testimonial can sometimes make a superb headline at the top of your sales letters. For example:

Dear Robert

"This technology beats anything we
have ever used before now."
G.W. Crammer, President, World Space Technology

Dear Robert

"Congratulations on producing the best cure
for hay fever that we have ever seen."
L.J. Sinnott, President, The World Hay Fever Foundation

Dear Robert

"I tell all my friends how good your
company is."
F. Burke, Chief Executive, Ionian Stock Exchange

Dear Robert

"Never once in 10 years has your
Techno-folder let us down."
P O'Connor, Chief Engineer, Sweetmount Paper Mills

SUMMARY OF CHAPTER 7:
HERE'S WHAT YOU SAY AND HOW YOU SAY IT

☐ Properly presented, a good testimonial can add considerable strength to your sales letter.

☐ The smaller, or more relatively-unknown, your company is, the more important it is for you to incorporate a good testimonial into your sales letter. In many ways, it works the same way as the magic word 'guarantee' works, because a good testimonial is effectively a guarantee.

☐ Most testimonials that are used in sales letters lack impact because they are too long or they are badly written.

☐ The best testimonials to use in a sales letter are those that are short and to the point and which promise a clear benefit to the reader.

☐ The most effective way for you to ask clients and friends for a good testimonial that you can use in your sales letter is to give them examples of the kind of testimonial that you would like to receive from them.

☐ The most effective positioning of a testimonial in your sales letter is in the second or third paragraph. But, sometimes, a testimonial can be so strong, and promise such an attractive benefit to your readers, that it may deserve pride of place in the very first paragraph of your sales letter.

☐ Testimonials can sometimes make very impactful headlines at the top of your sales letters.

8. GETTING THE TONE OF YOUR LETTER RIGHT

'Oh frabjous day! Callooh! Callay!'
He chortled in his joy.
Lewis Carroll, *Through the Looking Glass* (1865), Ch.1.

To write a really good sales letter, not only must you choose your words carefully, but also you need to 'talk' to your readers in the right tone of voice. As your readers read through your letter, they should be able to hear your voice conveying the tone of your sales message. The tone you adopt should be appropriate to the message you want to impart. And the secret of success with a good sales letter is to present your product or service to your readers in an interesting way … don't be a bore!

The secret of good copy – don't be a boar!

If, for example, you are writing to your readers about an exciting never-to-be-repeated bargain offer, then the tone of your copy should be exciting and fast and interesting.

On the other hand, if you are writing about rich, mellow, oak-aged whiskey, then your tone should be rich and melodious and interesting. If you are offering me a safe, secure, life assurance policy that will give me peace of mind for the rest of my days, then your tone should be comforting, reassuring and interesting. If you are writing to ask me to make a financial donation to help save starving children in a Third World country, your tone should be one of concern and encouragement ... and (wait for it!) your message should be interesting.

No matter what you are writing about, and no matter what tone (exciting, comforting, caring, reassuring, etc) you decide to use in your copy, your message must be **interesting to your reader**.

The reason why I am emphasising the words **'interesting to your reader'** is because you'd be surprised at how many uninteresting sales letters arrive on people's desks, and in their mail boxes, every single day of the year.

Of course, they're not meant to be uninteresting. In fact, the authors of these letters probably invested hours of their valuable time trying to make these letters sound as interesting as possible. Furthermore, they probably circulated their draft letters among their colleagues and peers and invited them to make suggestions as to what should be included in the letters and what should be excluded. And what they finally ended up with was a letter that all their colleagues and peers found interesting. That's super, if you are writing to your colleagues and peers. But it could be your death-knell if you are writing to customers and potential customers.

Because what your colleagues and peers find interesting may not be of interest – at all – to your customers and potential customers. And, if your customers find that your copy is boring and uninteresting, believe me, the response that you get to your sales letter will be boring and uninteresting too!

I've often attended briefing sessions with somewhat bewildered company managers whose sole purpose in asking me to attend the meeting is to find out *'What went wrong with our last direct mail campaign?'*. They tell me exactly what they have done.

They assure me that there is a proven need in the marketplace for their product or service. They impress me with the care they have taken and the expense they have incurred in choosing the right mailing list. They show me their flawlessly-printed brochures and their impeccably-produced personalised letters. They inform me that, without question, their product or service is competitively priced and they tantalise me with the irresistible free gift that they included in their offer. All in all, it's a wonderful sales pack – a veritable star in its own right!

But, despite all their collective efforts, care and investments, it didn't pull in a very good response. And for approximately five golden moments I am the undisputed star in the room, as all eyes look at me in anxious expectation to see what answer I will give to the key question that is on everyone's minds … *'What went wrong?'*.

Always, in situations like this, I go directly to the sales letter in the pack. I take my time and I read it carefully. In about eight out of every 10 situations like this, by the time I've finished reading the sales letter, I know what the answer to their question is. The answer is that the sales letter is unbelievably boring!

And when I gently mention to them that I, for one, don't find their sales letter very interesting, more often than not my comment is immediately dismissed out of hand and I'm politely told that I am, in effect, talking through my hat. I'm assured that while I, in my ignorance, might find the sales letter boring, the marketplace certainly wouldn't support my view. I'm reminded that I am but a mere wordsmith and that they are the experts in their own market.

Before I'm finally dismissed, I'm often asked have I any 'useful' observations to make as to what went wrong with their last mail pack. And I always stick to my guns and assure them that the most useful observation that I can possibly make to them is for me to repeat what I've said before: *'I don't find your sales letter very interesting'*. Uh Oh! In a situation like this, I'm not exactly playing at heading up the popularity stakes, am I?

But the truth is that, in situations like this, where I find a sales letter uninteresting to read, I genuinely do believe that this is where a major part of the problem lies. Of course, I may not understand the technical details and the finer points of the product or service on offer, but I do know a boring sales letter when I read one. You see, I can 'hear' it!

Sometimes it takes a complete outsider, someone who is unaware of subtle niceties and the finer points of your product or service, who is in the best position to tell you whether your sales letter is tuned in to the most important sales radio station of all.

THE RADIO STATION CALLED: WI-IFM

And WI-IFM stands for *'What's In It For Me?'*.

Tell me, your reader, *'What's in it for me?'* in your sales message and I promise you that I'll listen ever so carefully to what you are saying. And please tell me this quickly.

Because the faster I discover that there's something good for me in your sales message, the more you increase your chances of holding my attention and making me interested in what you are saying.

If a sales letter containing a useful, desirable and competitively-priced product or service is sent to the correct target group and it fails to produce a reasonable response, I generally find that the reason why the sales letter didn't work is because:

◊   You didn't hold my attention by telling me quickly *'What's in it for me?'*

◊   You didn't present your sales pitch to me in a way that was *'interesting to me'*.

Hold my interest in your sales letter by telling me as quickly as you can *'What's in it for me?'* if I agree to buy this product or service from you. It may not be always feasible, or even desirable, for you to explain this to me in the very first paragraph of your sales letter and that's okay with me. But don't leave it too late in your sales letter, because there is a danger that, if you leave it too late, my attention might have wandered elsewhere before I discover the answer to the all-important WI-IFM question.

One way for you to hold my attention is for you to use short sentences and paragraphs in your sales letters. You see, short sentences and short paragraphs make for speedy reading and, when people read something fast, they tend to concentrate more on what they are reading and they are less likely to be distracted by other things. The two key words are: 'quickly' and 'fast'. Tell me quickly what's in it for me and please ... make it fast!

This is what I call a 'good friends' approach.

Have you ever listened to two good friends, who haven't met each other for a while, talking to each other? Because, if you have, you'll have noticed something quite extraordinary. For starters, they both have so many interesting things to tell each other about that they both talk very fast!

It's exciting. They use short sentences! And approximately one in every four of their sentences starts with the word 'And': *'and wait till I tell you about this ...'*, *'and do you know what happened to me when ...?'*, *'and what'll you have to drink?'* and so on. Of course, they are both interested in catching up on the latest news about each other. But there's another reason why they are both talking so fast: it's because one doesn't want the other to interrupt what he or she is saying.

In the back of each person's mind is the belief that if the other person gets a 'leg in', so to speak, and starts talking, the listener might never get a word in edgeways for a while. So the person who has the floor talks very fast to hold on to the other's attention for as long as possible, and keep control of the way the conversation is going.

In Ireland, this doesn't put anybody at a disadvantage. Because Irish people, to the absolute amazement of just about everyone else in the world, all insist on talking at the same time. And while they assure you that they have magical powers that allow them to talk and listen at the same time, the truth of the matter is that they are only half paying attention to what you say to them. But it's great fun! It's exciting and it's interesting. And it makes for great company.

The reason why short sentences and short paragraphs work so effectively in sales letters is because they hold your attention in the fast-forward lane and don't give your thought process enough time to cut in and say *'Hey! I've read enough. I don't want to read any more!'*.

So, when you are writing your sales letter, you should keep my 'two friends' approach in mind and try to 'write the way you talk'.

WRITE THE WAY YOU TALK

Hey! Whoa! Hold On! Stop a minute! I've got four more important words that I'd like to add to this 'write the way you talk' formula. And I think you'll be amused when I tell you why.

Many, many years ago, I was invited to a somewhat remote part of the west of Ireland to give a presentation on *'How to write effective sales letters and brochures'* to a large group of wonderful people consisting of tradesmen: plumbers, welders, carpenters, plasterers and self-employed people.

They were a super audience. Things were going well. I could feel, and see, that they were listening carefully to everything I said. Then lo and behold, about half-way through my presentation, I announced to all the deeply reassuring news that the secret of writing a really good sales letter is to.... **WRITE THE WAY YOU TALK!**

Immediately, there was a silence in the room. Then, suddenly, a voice could be heard from somewhere at the back of the room saying:

'Jays*s, that f*cker up there says write the way you bleeding talk!'.

Huh! I didn't exactly mean write in *that* kind of talking language. There and then, I had to quickly amend my formula to: *'Write the way you talk ... to your best customer'*. By this I mean, keep it lively, fast-flowing, interesting and natural. Try not to use words that your readers may have difficulty understanding. And above all, avoid jargon or any kind of socially-unacceptable expletives!

AVOID JARGON

Tell me, do you know what a 'BRE' is? You don't! But everybody involved in the direct mail industry knows what a BRE is. You must be a sad person if you don't know what a BRE is.

But maybe you know what a 'PIF'd' loan account is? Say, you don't know this either! But everybody in the lending department of a bank knows what a PIF'd bank account is. Are you telling me that if your bank manager wrote to you, saying *'Congratulations, your loan is PIF'd'*, you wouldn't have a clue what he or she is writing to you about?

Sad!

Okay, let me try a third one: do you know what a 'FAQ' is? Aha! Now we may be getting somewhere, because quite a number of people do actually know that FAQ stands for a 'Frequently Asked Question'. But not everybody knows this.

Not everybody knows that a BRE stands for a Business Reply Envelope. And I'm willing to bet that most people don't know that a PIF'd loan account is a loan account that has been Paid In Full.

BRE ... FAQ ... PIF'd ... it's all jargon, you see.

The problem with using jargon in a sales letter is that some (sometimes, all!) of your readers might not have a breeze what you are talking about. This can have the off-putting effect of making some of your reader feel bewildered. And once a reader starts feeling intellectually-challenged, you weaken that all-important bond that you are trying to establish between yourself and your reader.

SPEEDY CONTRACTIONS

One very popular way of speeding up the flow of your copy, strengthening the bond between yourself and your readers, and consequently making it more difficult for your reader to stop reading, is to use contractions.

'Contractions' are another important characteristic of talking. Contractions are created when you run two words, usually a verb and an adverb, into each other. For example:

You will see	can be contracted to read	**You'll see**
I can not go	can be contracted to read	**I can't go**
He would like to	can be contracted to read	**He'd like to**
That is clever	can be contracted to read	**That's clever**
It is wrong	can be contracted to read	**It's wrong**

The reason why people use contractions when they are speaking is to keep their conversations lively, fast-flowing, interesting and natural. Try using contractions in your sales letters and immediately you'll find that your words flow faster across the page. But don't use contractions all the time!

Far and away the best effect is created in a sales letter when you only use contractions every now and again. For example:

> **'I am sorry, I can not** come this afternoon because **I can not** take time off from work to attend.'

Let's contract this sentence as much as possible so it reads:

> **'I'm** sorry, I **can't** come this afternoon because I **can't** take time off from work to attend.'

As you can see, in the second sentence, I've gone for the maximum number of contractions and I've ended up with a sentence that reads very much the way you would probably speak it. But, in written communications, rather than opt for the maximum number of contractions, I would much prefer you to present this sentence as follows:

> **I am sorry,** I **can't** come this afternoon because **I can not** take the time off from work to attend.

You see, I'm giving you a 'mix' as it were, and, in this case, I'm only using one contraction in the written sentence. Okay, there's no hard and fast rule about using contractions. But don't forget that really good sales copy should not only read right but should look right also. If you have too many contractions in your written communications, there is a danger that everything will look too laid-back.

It's a matter of striking the right balance for your readers.

SUMMARY OF CHAPTER 8:
HERE'S WHAT YOU SAY AND HOW YOU SAY IT

☐ You don't just read good copy – you hear it too!

☐ The best way for you to get your sales letter to sound right is to write the way you talk and keep everything moving forward at a fast pace.

☐ To speed up the rhythm of your copy, use short sentences and short paragraphs. Avoid jargon, because your reader might not immediately understand what it means and this, at best, will only slow things up. At worst, it means that you won't be able to hold their attention for very long.

☐ There is a radio station that everybody listens to 24-hours a day. It's called WI-IFM. This stands for *'What's in it for me?'.* If you want to hold on to your reader's attention, it's important for you to answer this question for them very early on in your sales letter. Don't leave it too late; otherwise, they may get bored and discard your letter long before they learn the answer to this important question.

☐ Use contractions to increase the tempo of your copy and to enhance the friendly talking tone of your sales letter.

9. INTRODUCING THE DREADED WORD 'AND'

> 'Will you walk a little faster?' said a whiting to a snail,
> There's a porpoise close behind us, and he's treading on my tail.'
> Lewis Carroll, *Alice's Adventures in Wonderland* (1865), Ch.10.

In every book, there has to be a controversial chapter and I guess this one is it! Because, in this chapter, I am going to tell you how to speed up the flow of your copy in a way that may have your school-teachers shaking their heads in despair.

As I mentioned to you in the last chapter, one sure-proof way of speeding up the rhythm of your copy is to write the way you talk and to use short – very short – sentences. Now, please don't get me wrong. Long, carefully-structured, sentences can be an absolute pleasure to read. How about this one ...

And they can create that wonderful feeling of timelessness and idyllic slow-moving summer days where the lazy bumble bees are buzzing from flower to flower and the gentle warm summer breeze is whispering over the rich green meadows, rippling the surface of the quiet mill pond which, in stark contrast to the mid-day heat looks, almost invitingly so, cool and calm and a perfect place for the miller's children – as John, the eldest of the present miller's large family, and the children of present miller's father before him, and, indeed, for as long as anyone in the neighbouring town land can remember – to play and to ...
(As you can see, this long single rambling sentence could on forever!)

But while long, sleepy, image-building and atmospherically-charged sentences like this may be a pleasure to read in novels about the rural countryside, they are not recommended for sales letters. The simple reason for this is that the sales letter copywriter must keep his/her readers awake and interested in his or her sales proposition!

Long, sleepy, rambling sentences can be a sales letter copywriter's greatest enemy because they can put your readers to sleep. This, of course, begs the question, what do you do when, on proofing your copy, you find that your sentences are too long?

HOW DO YOU SHORTEN A SENTENCE?

And the short simple answer that I will give you to this question is that, in the interest of speeding up the flow of your copy and writing the way you talk, never be afraid of breaking down a long sentence into two or more smaller sentences. Simply find a suitable place, somewhere near the middle of your sentence, to insert a full stop. And start a new sentence by inserting the word 'And'. After all, that's what you would do if you were talking.

Sometimes, when you go looking at an over-long sentence to see where's the most appropriate place for you to break it down into two shorter sentences, you'll find that there's already a handy little 'and' in the sentence. And all you have to do, to achieve the desired results, is insert a full stop immediately before the little 'and' and change the existing little 'and' into a big 'And'.

For example:

Dear Robert

The line-up of guest speakers for this year's Irish Copywriters Association's (ICA) Annual Conference, which is taking place in the Conrad Hotel on the 30th April, includes some of the best-known national and international speakers ever and all the indications are that this spectacular event will be fully booked out long before the final close-off date, 25th April, for accepting bookings.

You can quickly turn this long, and somewhat cumbersome sentence, into two more manageable sentences by simply ending the first sentence after the word 'ever' and starting the second sentence with the word 'And'.

Here's what you end up with:

Dear Robert

The line-up of guest speakers for this year's Irish Direct Copywriters Association's (ICA) Annual Conference, which is taking place in the Conrad Hotel on the 30th April, includes some of the best-known national and international speakers ever. And all the indications are that this spectacular event will be fully booked out long before the final close-off date, 25th April, for accepting bookings.

Another way of finding a suitable place to break up an overlong sentence into two shorter sentences is to put into practice what I preach when I advise you to 'write the way you talk' and read the sentence aloud.

What normally happens when you read a very long sentence out loud is that you find yourself running out of breath, and taking a quick gulp of air, somewhere along the way, for the simple reason that the sentence is too long for you to read aloud in one breath.

That's the place – the place where you gasp for breath – where you should try and put in your full stop, followed by the word 'And'. Yes! That's right! What I'm saying to you is never be afraid of starting a sentence with the word 'And'.

Whoa! Surely that can't be right! You can't start a sentence with the word 'And'.

Yes! You obviously had the same English teacher in school as I had. Do you remember being told that you must never – ever – start a sentence with the word 'And'. In fact, let's make no bones about it, you were told that a sentence beginning with the word 'And' was downright **bad grammar!**

And do you know something? It's not bad grammar at all! And if you don't believe me, what I want you to do before you retire to your bed tonight is go to your bookshelf beside your fireplace and take out that big, big book on it.

You know the book I'm talking about? I'm talking about the *Bible*, of course. And what I'd like you to do is settle down and read your *Bible* from cover to cover.

In it, you'll find sentences like:

> And now he is not just a slave, but more than a slave ... (St. Paul's letters to Philemon)
>
> And now he can help those who are tempted ... (Hebrews, 3)

Just about everywhere you look in the *Bible*, you'll find sentences beginning with the word 'And'.

And okay, okay, I know what you are now thinking. I remember giving a training course many years ago to a group of good God-fearing people in Northern Ireland. The moment I mentioned the *Bible*'s copious use of the word 'And', I could see that one of the lady participants was getting visibly agitated.

So I turned to her and invited her to have her say. Now I knew exactly where she was coming from. Furthermore, I knew exactly what she wanted to say. But somehow or other it came out all wrong. *'But ... but ... but'*, she spluttered, *'the Bible is only a ... fairy story!'*.

What! There was a stunned silence in the room. *'The Bible is only a fairy story!'*. Wow! All over the room I could see people getting upset. 'Flabbergasted' is perhaps the only word to describe the reaction in the room. And, of course, the poor lady who had made the comment was becoming highly embarrassed.

But – luckily – I could see immediately where she was coming from. I knew exactly what she was trying to say; only her problem was her somewhat unfortunate choice of words.

What she really meant was that the *Bible* is, beyond question, a good book. But the *Bible* never held itself up as being the paragon of the written English language. The *Bible*'s purpose is to communicate good news to the reader. And it does an excellent communications job in doing this. What my lady participant was trying to tell me was that I really hadn't picked a good example when I selected the *Bible* to support my case that it's okay to start a sentence with the word 'And'.

But I'd like you to do something else for me at this stage.

When you have finished reading your *Bible* from cover to cover, I'd like you to go to that very long line of books that are located on your bookshelf to the right of your *Bible*. You know the books I'm talking about?

What I'm talking about is the complete unabridged works of William Shakespeare – the 'Master' himself!

Select any book, any book at all. And, in it, you'll read things like:

And what shall I do in Illyria? (Shakespeare, *Twelfth Night*)

And my poor fool is hanged. (Shakespeare, *King Lear*, V.111)

All throughout Shakespeare's wonderful works, you'll find sentences beginning with the word 'And'. Furthermore, I believe that this is one of the reasons why Shakespeare's writings are so wonderfully free-flowing and melodious to read.

And believe you me: Shakespeare is the master of the English language. He's been hailed as the master for generations past. And, chances are, he'll be acclaimed as the master by many, many more generations to come.

Effectively, therefore, between the *Bible* and the works of William Shakespeare, you have God on your side and you have William Shakespeare on your side when you use 'And' to start a sentence. And you ain't going to get more powerful allies than this, are you?

Joking apart, however, have a careful look at the writings of many of today and yesterday's best-seller and blockbuster authors. I'm talking about Maeve Binchy, Stephen King, Evelyn Waugh ... and all those wonderful authors who write fabulously good books.

Look carefully and you'll quickly see that many of them start sentences with the word 'And'. In some cases, the 'and-count' can be as high as 1 in every paragraph, or even higher. It's one of the reasons why these books are such an effortlessly fast and enjoyable read.

It's always at this stage in my workshops that I see people looking at me with glazed eyes. And I know only too well what they are thinking. They are thinking things like:

` ... Robert is a very nice guy. Up to now, I've been learning a considerable amount of interesting things. I know he means well when he talks about starting a sentence with the word 'And'. So I'll just nod my head and smile at him ... and quietly forget all this nonsense about using 'And' to start a sentence. In any case, my boss, my company and my entire educational upbringing won't allow me to start a sentence with the word 'And'.'

All right! But let me tell you one last interesting thing. One of the real beauties of using the word 'And' at the beginning of a sentence is that, not only does it definitely speed up the flow of the copy, but – and this is important – most people will never even notice that you are using it.

For example, when you were reading your newspaper this morning did you notice any sentences in it beginning with the word 'And'? You probably didn't. But what about the Editorial section of your newspaper, which is usually one of the most carefully-written, and grammatically-correct, section of any newspaper? Did you notice any sentences beginning with 'And' in the Editorial? Now, of course, I can't guarantee this but, if I were a betting man, I'd be prepared to bet you a Mars Bar that if you go back and have another look, you'll probably find at least one sentence in the editorial, or leading article, of this morning's newspaper (any newspaper) which begins with the word 'And'.

It's not that sentences beginning with 'And' suddenly appear by magic on second reading, it's just that, if you're like most newspaper readers, you never noticed it first time around.

Rest assured that it's perfectly good grammar to start a sentence with the word 'And'. Furthermore, this is a very useful method of shortening sentences and making the copy of your sales letter flow faster and smoother.

SUMMARY OF CHAPTER 9:
HERE'S WHAT YOU SAY AND HOW YOU SAY IT

- ☐ If your letter is a 'fast read', your readers will retain more of your sales message. They will also find it hard not to read your entire letter.

- ☐ Long sentences will slow up your readers and, if at all possible, should be avoided.

- ☐ Many writers find it difficult to keep their sentences short. One way of shortening an overlong sentence, and increasing the rhythm of the copy, is to break down the long sentence into two shorter sentences and to start the second sentence with the word 'And'.

☐ Purists will say that you should never start a sentence with the word 'And'. But some of the greatest and most popular writers of all times have been more than happy to use 'And' to start sentences. Likewise, some of the greatest direct mail letters of all times contain sentences that start with the word 'And'. It speeds up the flow of the copy and brings you closer to writing the way you talk.

☐ If you are unhappy about using the word 'And' to start a sentence in your sales letter, don't do it. Remember, the reason why I introduced the concept to you in the first place is to give you a handy writer's tool for shortening overlong sentences. Careful editing and re-writing of overlong sentences will also achieve the same objective; which is ... *'Keep your sentences short!'*.

10. GETTING THE APPEARANCE OF YOUR LETTER RIGHT

'Curiouser and curiouser!', cried Alice.
Lewis Carroll, *Alice's Adventures in Wonderland* (1865), Ch.1.

'Looking good' is an important part of your overall strategy for capturing and holding your readers' attention on the words that you write.

Keep in mind what I said earlier about how you don't just 'read' good sales copy, you 'hear' it too. Furthermore, you **'see'** it too! So not only must your words be carefully chosen, and your tone as friendly and persuasive as you can make it, but the type font and the layout of your letter must also be as attractive as possible for your readers' eyes.

Let me give you a practical example of how important it is for you to keep up your appearances in your letter. Have a look at the paragraph on the next page and, before you start reading it, ask yourself the question: Does this paragraph look attractive?

You've already taken the first step by successfully completing your ECDL Certificate Course with ABC. Your next step to gaining an ADVANCED ECDL certificate is easy. It's easy because you're familiar with the friendly teaching environment at ABC and you'll be surprised at how quickly we can help you advance towards being awarded with this valuable Certificate. It makes sense too because ABC has one of the highest success rates in the country with the ECDL course. Not only are we a winner of the ECDL Best Practice Award, but also we're the first training centre in the North East to become an ECDL Advanced Test Centre. So the quicker you sign up to do this course with ABC the faster you'll have that very useful Advanced ECDL Certificate. It's useful, because it will really advance your CV. It will immediately help you to advance your earning power. And talking about money – you'll find that ABC is one of the most competitively-priced computer training centres in the country. It's also useful because it will advance your job mobility – and that's important now that our economy is slowing down somewhat. Plus, of course, there's a huge sense of personal achievement in successfully completing this valuable certificate course. Not to mention all the additional useful, practical things that you'll learn about computers. Remember, one of the reasons why the ADVANCED ECDL is so universally well regarded is because it's an extremely well structured course.

No! It doesn't look attractive at all. In fact, what does that last paragraph remind you of?

It reminds me of school! To me it brings back memories - bad memories – of those long unwieldy passages of Virgil that we used to have to memorise for our Classical Studies teacher. In an odd old way. it also reminds me of 'lines'! *'Take a hundred lines as punishment'*, teacher used to say. And you'd spend the rest of the night ruining your handwriting skills for life by trying to write as fast as you possibly could a hundred lines of *'I must not try to imitate the teacher in class'*, or whatever.

So before I even start to read a long paragraph like the sample paragraph that I have given you, I have bad memories – bad vibes! This is something that, at all costs, you should try to avoid giving your readers. Because, if a reader gets into a negative frame of mind by simply looking at the appearance of your letter, you have considerably weakened the foundations upon which you are so carefully building your sales message.

Another thing that you should keep in mind is that long paragraphs in a letter not only look ugly, but they are an absolute plague to read. It's very difficult to concentrate for any length of time on something that looks ugly and boring. Your whole instinct is to quickly move on to something that looks more lively and interesting. This moving-on-quickly process is called 'skip reading'. And most of us, I'm afraid, to a greater or lesser extent, are 'skip readers' in our reading habits, particularly when it comes to reading sales letters.

That's why my 'general' advice to you over the last few chapters of this book has been to keep your paragraphs as short and as interesting looking as possible. Now, I'm going to be specific: Try! Try very hard never to exceed **six lines** in any paragraph.

I know that this isn't always easy. But it's worth your while to try. Because if you can successfully limit ALL your paragraphs to six lines or less, you'll enrich the appearance of your letter and enhance the 'readability' of your letter as well.

Many companies fall into the 'long paragraph' trap in their sales letters. You see, sometimes you have so many good things to say that you find that you simply haven't got enough space in your letter to tell your reader everything that *you* want them to know about your products and services.

So, in the interest of not leaving anything out, you end up squeezing in as much information and detail as you can into long paragraphs. The result is that, sometimes, your strongest selling points are lost in a myriad of words in an overlong and ugly-looking paragraph that the skip-reader will happily hoppity-skip over.

And that's not all the bad news!

I've done this in the past, and I'm sure you've done it too! Have you ever found yourself looking at a paragraph in a draft sales letter and deciding this is too long? And instead of editing it down, which is what you should do, you try and fool your reader into thinking it's shorter by making the size of your type font smaller. The end result is a long paragraph of tiny – tiny – type!

Don't ever be tempted to do this. Long paragraphs of tiny type are a skip-reader's paradise; they will simply skip over them even faster. And all your wonderful words of wisdom, and all your carefully-presented product benefits and features may never even be seen by the skip-reader.

Keep your paragraphs short and pay careful attention to the size of the type font that you use, otherwise you could find that a sizeable number of your readers won't bother reading your sales message, no matter how attractive and persuasive your words are.

WHAT TYPE ARE YOU?

The type font that you use in your sales letter plays an important role in helping you to achieve the right 'appearance' for your sales letter. Have a look at these different type fonts, which are all printed in 11 point type size, and see if you notice anything in particular about them.

1. Look at me, I'm written in a serif type font. (Times New Roman.)

2. Look at me, I'm written in a sans-serif type font. (Arial Narrow)

3. Look at me, I'm written in a serif type font. (Courier)

4. Look at me, I'm written in a sans-serif type font. (Helvetica)

5. Look at me, I'm written in a serif type font. (Bookman Old Style)

6. Look at me, I'm written in a sans-serif type font. (Abadi MT Condense)

7. Look at me, I'm written in a serif type font. (Poor Richard)

8. Look at me, I'm written in a sans-serif type font. (Verdana)

9. Look at me, I'm written in a serif type font. (Georgia)

10. Look at me, I'm written in a sans-serif type font. (VAG Rounded Th)

Now I'm sure that the very first thing that will catch your eye as you look at the different fonts in the 10 lines above is that some of them appear as if they are printed in a larger type size than others. Some look bolder than others too. The fact is that they are **all** printed in 11 point font size.

But hey! If they are all printed in the same font size (11 point), how come there's such a marked variation in the size of the different type fonts that are in the above list? The short answer to this question is: That's just the way it is, I'm afraid.

You see, some fonts are designed to be bigger than others and some are much more spaced-out than others. It's no big deal, but it's something that you should know: some fonts are bigger and clearer than others.

That's why if you ever ask a printer or lettershop (a company that specialises in producing sales letters and direct mail promotional packs) to look after the preparation of your sales letters for you, you should always give them very specific instructions about which **font** you want them to use in your letters and, in addition, you should very specifically tell them which **font size** you want them to use.

And even then, don't leave anything to chance! You see, different computer software manufacturers can do different things to type fonts. It's always wise to look at the printer or lettershop's final draft of your letter before you press the 'go-ahead' button. Make sure that their computer system produces your letter exactly as you want your customers to read it.

WHAT'S THE BEST FONT & SIZE TO USE?

Most business letters are typed in 12 point font size. But be careful with your font sizes. One glance at the selection of type fonts above will immediately show you that, in relative terms, Times is a very small type font compared with, let's say, Courier or Helvetica and that Poor Richard is even smaller.

So, while your company may have a house-rule that all letters should be typed up in 12 point size for clarity of reading, it's not the point size on its own that guarantees what the end product will look like. The actual font that you use will also play a very important role in presenting your written communications to your target group.

Far and away, my preferred font for use in a sales letter is Times New Roman. It's a very clear distinctive type font. And because it is a serif type font, it's a fast-flowing and easy font for just about everybody to read.

'Serif!', 'Sans serif?'. You'll notice that I keep on referring to these two expressions in my list of type fonts above. So the question that we now need to address ourselves to is: What on earth is a serif?

WHAT ON EARTH IS A SERIF?

Put another way ... when I tell you that some of the fonts in my list above have a serif and that others have no serif (*sans-serif* is the French for 'without a serif'), what am I referring to? What difference does it make to reading?

The best way I can describe this to you is to take the humble 'T', and contrast a Times New Roman 'T' (a serif font) with an Arial Narrow 'T' (a sans-serif font).

Look at me ... I'm a Times New Roman 'T' with a serif	Look at me ... I'm an Arial Narrow 'T' with no serif (sans serif)
T	**T**
Serif	**Sans serif**

Now, do you see that little horizontal line, highlighted within a circle, at the bottom of the 'T' in the serif box above? That little horizontal line is called a 'serif'. As you can see, the 'T' in the sans-serif box above has no horizontal line or serif.

Let's try another little example. Let's take a 'K'.

Look at me ... I'm a Times New Roman 'K' with a serif	Look at me ... I'm an Arial Narrow 'K' with no serif (sans serif)
K	**K**
Serif	**Sans serif**

As you can see, the 'K' in the Times New Roman serif font is almost sexy because, not only does it have little horizontal lines at the foot of the letter, but it has them at the top of the letter as well. Contrast this with the stark, pure, vertical simplicity of the Arial sans serif **K**.

Those little horizontal lines are called serifs. Serif type fonts have a considerable antiquity – they developed from handwriting using quills or wedge-tipped pens. Sans-serif fonts are more modern. Which looks nicer?

I have to confess that I prefer the artistic simplicity of the sans-serif font. It's pure, uncluttered vertical lines are a joy to look at compared with the somewhat old-fashioned horizontal fussiness of, let's say, the Times New Roman serif font.

But hold it! Wait a minute! Stop! Pay attention! Let's not get carried away with artistic simplicity and suchlike. Do you know that serif fonts have the decided advantage of being far quicker for most people to read than san-serif fonts?

If you think about it, this makes good common sense. When you are reading, unless you are reading Chinese, your eyes move on a horizontal line from left to right. And those little horizontal serifs help your eyes to follow the natural eye-reading movement. With serifs, word shapes are more distinctive and, with the aid of those horizontal little serif bars, your eyes skim merrily along the line in an easy forward-moving momentum.

Sans-serif fonts don't have these little horizontal tramlines for your eyes to follow. The shape of the letters is vertical (up-down) with the result that it's pulling up against the natural horizontal movement of the reading eye ... **it's slowing you down.**

So my advice to anyone who wants to write a very persuasive sales letter is, use a serif type font, preferably Times New Roman, in your sales letters. Serif fonts are faster, easier and friendlier to read. Independent tests have shown that, if you ask someone to read a page of copy in serif type and a page of copy in sans serif type, they will recall more of contents of the serif type page than they will of the sans-serif page. That's because they can read it faster and ... 'the faster you read, the more you absorb'.

I have a little ditty that I use in my writing workshops and it goes like this:

The faster you read, the more you absorb
The more you absorb, the more you like
The more you like, the more you buy
The more you buy, the more you ...

So, not only is the serif font text easier to read, but it increases your response too!

And Times, or the many different derivatives of Times, such as Times Roman or Times New Roman, is among the most popular fonts used in businesses all over the world. That's why I always advise my clients, and I strongly advise you as well, to use a Times font in all your sales letters.

Interestingly enough, many successful charity appeal letters use a serif type font. And more often than not, it's not Times that they use ... they use the old-fashioned Courier font! Some professional fund-raisers will tell you that the open manual-typewriter style of the courier font is not only much easier to read (particularly for the 45+ age group who are super charity supporters) but it gives a far more intimate and hands-on appearance to the appeal message.

The hidden suggestion underlying the use of the old-fashioned manual-typewriter Courier font is that the charity simply doesn't have enough money to afford a computer to write their appeal letters with.

I'm not going to dispute this logic, as I have used Courier very successfully in charity appeals over the years. But lately, I've stopped using it, because I'm of the opinion that the key 45+ age group is no longer as impressed as it used to be by the manual-typewriter appearance of the Courier font. After all, this is the age group that created the PC. They've long ago moved on from manual typewriters and Courier fonts.

Before I move on, let me say a few words in defence of the beautiful-looking sans-serif fonts. In small point sizes, sans-serif fonts are much clearer to read than serif fonts. Also, it is said that young people, who have been exposed to more sans-serif fonts than, perhaps, older people, have no difficulty at all reading sans-serif fonts. Young people who are very familiar with email and telephone text messages feel very much at ease with sans-serif fonts. When you think about it, the default on most email messages is the thin, sans serif Arial Narrow font.

But! Be careful! Because there is less variation in the shape of the letters in the vertically-oriented sans-serif font, if you ask your reader, regardless of his or her age, to read too much of it, or if you present them with a big unwieldy unbroken block of sans-serif text, your message can look very, very, tedious indeed.

And if your message looks tedious you are, from a sales letter copywriter's viewpoint, creating problems with a big 'P' for yourself when you are trying to sell your products, services or concepts to your readers. Because nobody likes reading a tedious-looking message.

'Tedious', according to my thesaurus, means: dull, boring, burdensome, lifeless, ponderous, heavy, tiresome, wearisome. Yikes! Imagine reading a sales letter that fits even *one* of these descriptions.

TYPEFACES REVEAL PERSONALITY TRAITS

I've always been interested in fonts in all shapes and sizes, so some time ago an article in the *Daily Telegraph* caught my eye. 'Typefaces, it informed me, reveal personality traits'.

The article (*Daily Telegraph*, 24 May 2001) went on to say, in effect, that the computer typeface used in an email or letter can tell the reader more about the writer's personality than the actual words that the written message contains.

According to Dr. Arik Sigman, a psychologist who investigated the links between personality traits and typefaces, Courier font, regarded as the 'anorak of fonts', is used by older administration staff secretaries, who harbour latent nostalgia for the era of typewriters and carbon paper, and old school journalists who associate it with whiskey, cigarettes, late nights and goose-neck lamps.

Serif styles, the article went on to say, such as Times New Roman, showed a compromise between the old and new, conjuring up images of trustworthiness that have made them a favourite with solicitors.

Sans serif styles, such as Arial, were the 'sensible pair of shoes of print', while fashion-conscious 'pop chicks' used curvy fonts such as Georgia.

Here, let me give them all to you:

Courier	Anorak font, stuck in the past
Helvetica	Modern, in touch with contemporary issues
Times New Roman	Trustworthy and a link between new and old
Arial	A safe choice, like a pair of sensible shoes
Georgia	Soft and curvy, popular with 'pop chicks'
Comic Sans	Attention-seeking, nauseating
Handwriting font	The worst offender - presumes familiarity

Source: *Daily Telegraph*, 24 May 2001.

And, to add to my enjoyment, the *Daily Telegraph* article then went on to ask me this earth-shattering question: *'Guess which font is used by Prince Charles?'*.

The answer to this question is, of course, Helvetica – modern, in touch with contemporary issues. Mind you, Helvetica is a sans-serif font that is a difficult font to concentrate on for any length of time. But I guess, Prince Charles' communication advisors are very much aware of this and you'll probably find that he keeps his written communications short and very much to the point.

The newspaper industry cottoned on to the easy-readability advantage of the serif font a long time ago. You see, its readers are the lifeblood of a newspaper. If the readers don't enjoy reading a particular newspaper, they may stop buying it. And if this happens, very quickly the newspaper will go out of business.

For reasons of space-economy, most newspapers are printed in relatively small type. The headlines are big, but the main-body copy of the average newspaper is quite small. So the problem that one major national newspaper had to face up to in the past was: *'How can we keep – and hold – our readers' interest when we want them to read small type?'*.

The answer to this question is that they used a serif font to make their newspaper more reader-friendly. Over time, they carefully developed and refined their serif font, until they achieved the level of perfection in legibility and ease in reading that they were looking for. And, of course, they named this very distinctive type font after their own newspaper. They called it Times, the name of the newspaper.

Most newspapers that arrive on my desk use a Times font in the main-body copy. But have you ever noticed how some newspapers, particularly the tabloids, use a crisp san-serif font in the HEADLINES!

The purpose of the headline in a newspaper is to capture your attention, encourage you to stop awhile and read more. For example, most people would be tempted to stop and read more of an article headed up with this headline:

Hitler did it, so can you!

Have a look at a few newspapers, particularly the increasingly popular tabloids, and see for yourself how cleverly they mix their fonts. They use big slow-moving sans-serif fonts in the headlines, which are usually short and to the point. And then, in the news feature or article that follows, they use a small serif font that is ideal for legibility and for comfortable reading.

Try using this combination of a sans-serif font in the headline and a serif font in the main body copy of your next sales letters, and I think you'll immediately find that more people are reading (and remembering) your letters.

SUMMARY OF CHAPTER 10:
HERE'S WHAT YOU SAY AND HOW YOU SAY IT

- ☐ In addition to getting the words and the tone of your letter right, you must also pay careful attention to the appearance of your letter.

- ☐ Few people will enjoy the prospect of having to read a boring looking sales letter that contains long and unwieldy paragraphs. So keep your paragraphs short, and don't be tempted to 'cheat' by using a very small type size in order to cram more words into a short-looking paragraph.

- ☐ Use a serif type font in all your sales letters, preferable a Times font. The serif helps your reader to read faster and, consequently, they will retain more of your sales message in their memory.

☐ It's worth remembering that the default font on most email message programmes is Arial Narrow. This is a sans serif font. which is fine for headlines and short paragraphs but, in longer paragraphs, it can be tedious to read and hard to concentrate on.

☐ Remember, words on their own don't make up a good sales letter – it's what you say ... how you say it ... and how it **looks** that define the parameters of your very persuasive sales letter.

11. Eye-Read Your Message

> He thought he saw an Elephant
> That practised on a fife:
> He looked again, and found it was
> A letter from his wife.
> Lewis Carroll, *Sylvie and Bruno* (1889), Ch.5.

You now know that a serif helps the eyes to move quickly and accurately along the different lines of your copy from left to right. But the reading-eye does more than just move from left to right across the page. It also moves from the top of the page to the bottom.

This is all very logical. But it also has an interesting little message for the sales letter copywriter. Have a look at the sample address and opening paragraph of the letter below and I'll explain to you what exactly happens when people open a letter and start reading it.

 Ms Hazel McCoy
Honeysuckle Cottage
Briar Road
Bushtown
Forestfield
Date

Dear Hazel

As a valued customer of ours we'd like you to know that...

The very first place that your readers' eye will go to when they open this letter is the top left-hand corner, where the name and address is normally positioned. This happens in a fraction of a second and most people don't even notice that they are doing it. Part of the reason why people do this is because they are doing a quick check to make sure that they not reading somebody else's letter. It's the very first thing that your reader will look at, so it's essential that you have their correct name and address.

Now I had an interesting little experience some years ago that I'd like to share with you now.

I have no idea what I was wearing. I can't even remember what I purchased. But whatever I did, or said, when I visited a well-known international department store some time ago, I ended up on their mailing list. This doesn't surprise me at all, because as a copywriter for the direct marketing industry, I always make a point of trying to get my name on as many mailing lists as possible.

You see, I like to receive lots of sales letters and I always make it my business to read these letters carefully to see whether I can learn anything new from them. That's because I'm always on the look out for new ways of saying things or clever ideas that I can develop for myself.

Sometimes, if you mix part of an idea from one letter with a suggestion or a headline from another, you can end up with a very interesting concept of your own. That's why, if anybody ever asks me if I would like to go on their mailing list, my answers is always 'Yes'!

So I guess I must have said 'Yes' to somebody in that well-known department store when they asked me whether I would like to go on their mailing list. So far so good, but from that point on something must have gone decidedly wobbly.

You see, mine is a very unusual name: Robert Hayes-McCoy. It's not *my* fault that I have a long hyphenated name like this. It's a name that has been in my family for generations and I don't think any of us have ever really given it much thought. Now maybe I looked a bit odd that day when I was shopping in the department store, or perhaps I was talking in a squeaky voice, or whatever.

But the upshot was that within a very short period of time I received a letter from the store addressed to: **Ms Hazel McCoy!**

To make matters worse, the letter went on to say: *'Dear Hazel ... as a valued customer of ours, we'd like you to know that, etc, etc.'*.

Wow! Talk about digging a hole! Despite the flawlessly-presented letter, containing rich words of comfort and welcome, it was quite obvious that the store hadn't a breeze who I was. Actually, it was all quite harmless and amusing. Because as the months went by I had great fun reading all the special *'Dear Hazel'* offers I received.

But the point being made here is that, if you get your reader's name wrong, or if you spell it incorrectly, it will be the very first thing that he or she will notice when they open your letter. And once your reader sees that you haven't a breeze who you are writing to, no amount of expensive personalisation or intimate offers will undo the damage done.

The reality of the situation, as anyone in the direct mail business will tell you, is that it's almost impossible to keep a database of names and addresses 100% accurate. But you should always try hard to get it accurate. Keep in mind that every inaccurately-addressed letter is a waste of an opportunity. It could even be worse than this, because it could convey an entirely negative image of your company to your reader.

So try your level best to get names and addresses correct. If you have any doubt at all about the accuracy of an address, or the correct way to spell a potential client's name, my advice to you is either take it out of your mailing list entirely or check it out at once! If the contact is important to you, it's worth your while to pick up the telephone and call the receptionist at his or her company and ask the receptionist to verify for you the correct spelling of a name, position in the company or the correct address of the person you want to send your sales letter to. This telephone call will only take you a minute or two to make and you'll be amazed at how helpful and friendly company receptionists can be when you ask them to help you with matters like this.

Now that we know the very first place where your readers' eye will go to when they open your sales letter, I'd like to show you what happens next. This time I'm going to use a mini-sample letter, which is addressed to Mr John Murphy, Managing Director of J. Murphy & Company.

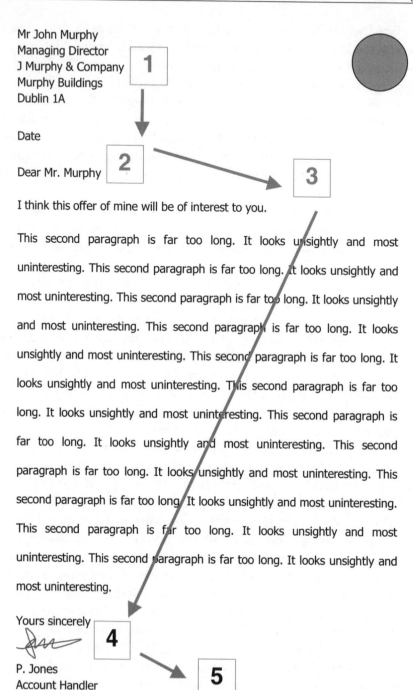

Mr John Murphy
Managing Director
J Murphy & Company
Murphy Buildings
Dublin 1A

1

Date

Dear Mr. Murphy
2

3

I think this offer of mine will be of interest to you.

This second paragraph is far too long. It looks unsightly and most uninteresting. This second paragraph is far too long. It looks unsightly and most uninteresting. This second paragraph is far too long. It looks unsightly and most uninteresting. This second paragraph is far too long. It looks unsightly and most uninteresting. This second paragraph is far too long. It looks unsightly and most uninteresting. This second paragraph is far too long. It looks unsightly and most uninteresting. This second paragraph is far too long. It looks unsightly and most uninteresting. This second paragraph is far too long. It looks unsightly and most uninteresting. This second paragraph is far too long. It looks unsightly and most uninteresting. This second paragraph is far too long. It looks unsightly and most uninteresting. This second paragraph is far too long. It looks unsightly and most uninteresting. This second paragraph is far too long. It looks unsightly and most uninteresting. This second paragraph is far too long. It looks unsightly and most uninteresting.

Yours sincerely

4

5

P. Jones
Account Handler

PS. Now you can see, Mr Murphy, why I'd like to offer you a million Euro next Friday morning at 10am.

1 & 2: Everything, so far, in the above sample letter is okay. We've got John Murphy's name, company, position in company and address details all correct.

Before we move away from the salutation line, *'Dear Mr. Murphy'*, let's quickly address the thorny question of how familiar should you be in your salutation? Some people, perhaps many people, would much prefer to address Mr. Murphy as *'John'* in the salutation line.

Of course, *'Dear John'* is more intimate than *'Dear Mr. Murphy'* but, if you've never met John Murphy, or if you know very little about him, is it wise to use *'Dear John'* in your sales letter to him? I don't believe it is.

I guess it's all about human behaviour and territorial space. A territory is a defended space. Some people don't like strangers addressing them by their first name, because they feel that it is an intrusion on their territorial space. Others don't mind this at all; in fact, they may be flattered to find that a total stranger wants to be on friendly first-name terms with them. But is it worth the risk? Especially, when I don't think anybody – anybody at all – objects to a total stranger addressing him or her in the more formal *'Dear Mr. Murphy'* style.

The risk of intruding on your reader's territorial space increases significantly when it comes to using nicknames or pet names. For example if you know that John Murphy is always called *'Johnny'* by his family ... don't even think about it! I'm not even going to tell you what you're not to think about, just don't do it. Okay, here it is ... don't ever use nicknames or pet names in your sales letters to total strangers.

The best approach, and far and away the safest approach, is the more formal approach: *'Dear Mr. Murphy'*. Over time, when Mr. Murphy gets to know you better, after you've written him a number of different sales letters, you might – just might – opt to adopt the informal *'Dear John'* approach. But be careful with this. My advice to you is to play safe. If you are like most people, you tend to back off if a stranger stands too closely beside you and intrudes in your personal space. The last thing you want is for someone who receives a sales letter from you to back off before they even read your first paragraph because you've been too familiar with them in your salutation.

3. After moving from '1' to '2', the eye quickly moves down to '3', which is the opening paragraph of your letter.

This, as you now know, is the most important paragraph of your entire letter. This is the make or break point of your reader's attention. This is the point where your reader decides – decides in a flash – whether or not this letter is worth reading. So it's very important for you to get your opening right! Say something interesting. Grab his or her attention by using one of the magic words in your opening sentence. Better still, try and use the platinum word 'You'. Now let's suppose the opening paragraph is a simple one-liner which reads:

'Dear Mr. Murphy, I'd like to give you a million Euro!'

Most people who read an opening sentence like this, even the most sceptical, especially if the million Euro offer is addressed to them by name, will do something very interesting at this stage. What they will do is immediately glance down (or flip over the page, if your sales letter contains more than a single page) to find out: *'Who exactly wants to give me a million Euro?'*. They will look at the signature. And, in the case of the above letter, they will immediately see that the signature is a squiggle!

'Squiggle' wants to give me a million Euro! Uh Oh! Things are beginning to go downhill very quickly. Because 'Squiggle' neither looks nor sounds too convincing, does it? That's the problem with a squiggly signature – it send out all the wrong signals. It suggests that the person who is signing this letter:

◊   Couldn't be bothered spending too much time on it

◊   Is hiding behind a squiggle

◊   Is somewhat offhand or not being very honest about the offer being made to you.

4. A clear open blue-ink signature not only stands out clearly on the page but also sends out powerful messages to the reader – messages of openness and honesty. Had there been a nice big open and honest-looking signature here, I'm sure Mr. Murphy would have been much more impressed with that one million Euro offer in the opening paragraph.

Now I've no idea what you, my reader, are like. But I'd like you to know that when I was a schoolboy I used to spend hours ... and hours ... and hours practising my signature. You see I wanted to develop an impressive-looking squiggle. After all, all the film stars in those days used squiggles. And all the grown-ups that I knew who signed cheques used squiggles for their signature. So I wanted a squiggle too!

Although I'm not as proficient at it as I used to be, I can still do that squiggle of mine. It looks something like this:

I carried that squiggle with me from my school days into university and right up to my early working days, until I began to work in direct marketing. And one of the very first lessons that I learned in direct marketing was that a blue-ink signature can pull a better response to a sales letter than a black-ink one does. So, for a while, I took great care to ensure that all my squiggles were **blue** squiggles.

Then I discovered that the more legible one's signature, the more positive the message it conveys to your reader – a message of being open, honest and having nothing to hide. So I developed this new signature:

And from the moment I started using my new signature, I knew I was doing the right thing. People commented favourably upon it. Some even went so far as to ask me why I put two little dots under the small 'c' of McCoy? For those of you who don't know the answer to this question, let me tell you that those two little dots represent the missing 'a' in Mac. Presumably at one stage in the family history we were 'The Real MacCoys!' And then some distant ancestor of mine decided to drop the 'a' in Mac in preference to 'Mᶜ'. Whoever he was, he obviously didn't anticipate the arrival of computers that come pre-loaded with software containing a set of standard fonts. Because nowhere in my entire computer font selection can I find a little 'c' with those two all-important dots underneath it.

But that new signature of mine certainly did catch on. So much so that, when the great day came for me to register my own company, I decided to use my signature as my company logo. I now use it everywhere. Today, my squiggle is nothing more than a dim and distant memory of the past.

So, if you are in the habit of signing your name with a squiggle, my advice to you is (even if you want to hang on to your squiggle for everything else in your life that requires your signature) change it to a more open, honest and legible one in your important sales letters.

5. Something very interesting happens after your reader's eye has glanced down at your signature. Since all of us read communications in the English language from 'left to right' across the page and down the page from 'top to bottom', the natural tendency for the eye is to move down from the signature to the PS underneath. Hence there is a strong likelihood that, if your opening paragraph is good, the eye will look down to the signature and then immediately move further down the page to read the PS. That's why the PS can be the second most important part of your letter after the first paragraph.

This is why it's so important for you to take care to ensure that the PS is not wasted. Far too many sales letters with a PS that arrive on my desk contain very weak sales messages in the PSs. The say things like *'Now you know where to go ...'* or *'Call us soon!'*, or whatever. This, in my view, is a waste of a sales opportunity. It's certainly a waste of space in the second most important part of your sales letter.

You should use your PS to say something vibrant and interesting. Use it to offer yet another valuable benefit. Or use it, like I've done in my sample mini-letter above, to draw my reader's attention right back up into the main body copy of my letter.

> PS. Now you can see, Mr. Murphy, why I'd like to offer you a million Euro next Friday morning at 10am.

Chances are that Mr Murphy will take one look at that PS and go right back up to the top and read my entire letter very carefully.

But before I go on let me ask you – yet again – a very important question. And my question to you, in case you haven't already guessed it is this: *'Did you have the same English teacher as I had?'*.

DID YOU HAVE MY ENGLISH TEACHER?

If you had the same English teacher as I had, you'll probably remember these words: *'You should never – ever – use a PS in your letters. Because a PS,'* as my teacher would say, *'is an indication of an untidy mind. It's a sure-proof sign that you haven't structured your letter carefully enough. It means that you've forgotten to include something important. So you are putting it in at the end.'*

Absolutely correct! That's why just about everybody reads a PS in a letter. They want to know what it was that you forgot to include in your letter? What was so important that you couldn't leave it out? But can I give you just a little word of warning about the PS? It's at this stage in my copywriting workshops that I generally notice the participants writing furiously. What they are all writing in their notepads – believe me, I've checked it time and time again – is a little message to themselves saying, in effect: *'Every good sales letter should have a PS'*. All I can say to you here is *'please be careful'*.

In Ireland, and I'm sure the same thing happens in just about every other country that uses direct mail, as the number of sales letters and direct mail letters began to increase, the universal message went out that: *'All good direct mail letters should have a PS'*.

Again and again in my workshops, I find myself being taken to task for showing examples of wonderful sales letters – superb letters – which, horror of horrors, don't have the requisite PS at the end of them. Invariably, someone will put up their hand and triumphantly make the point that my demonstration letter couldn't possibly be a good letter because it doesn't have a PS in it. Clients who commission me to write their sales letters sometimes gently reprove me if I decide not to put a PS at the end of their letter. They honestly believe that a sales letter without a PS is not a proper sales letter at all. They want a PS and they feel short-changed if I don't give them one.

Talking of being short-changed on the PS reminds me of a hilarious episode that I read in that magnificent book written by John McGahern, *That They May Face the Rising Sun.*

> One of the people in McGahern's book is a copywriter like myself, who (for reasons that I won't go into here) is asked to write an important letter for a farmer friend of his. During the course of their conversation, the farmer began to reflect on a humorous little situation that used to be commonplace in rural Ireland of the old days. In those days, many people received important letters – letters with much-needed money attached to them – from other members of their family who had emigrated overseas. And, of course, the grateful recipient would have to send back a reply letter to acknowledge the safe arrival of the money, which sometimes was the only source of finance that kept them on the right side of the poorhouse.

> In those days, if you couldn't write, you went to the local schoolmaster and asked him to write your important letter for you. Of course, the schoolmaster was only too willing to oblige. It seems that the accepted system was that the schoolmaster would charge a fee for this service, like a lawyer.

> When he had the letter written, the schoolmaster would read it back to the client. And he'd ask if they would like him to add a personal little PS message at the end of the letter for them. Once it was established that there was no extra charge for adding on a PS at the end of the letter, the client would be happy enough with the idea. And he or she would ask the schoolmaster to write: *'PS. Please excuse bad writing and spelling!'*

> Can you imagine the look on the schoolmaster's face as he added this PS to his carefully written letter? It appears that, at that time, many people believed that this was the correct message to put in a PS at the bottom of a letter. You see, they heard it read out in other letters and they didn't want their own letter to look in any way inferior.

I'm sharing this delightful little story with you because I want you to know that, despite what everybody else may do in his or her sales letters, you don't always have to have a PS at the end of your 'very persuasive sales letter'.

My advice to you is, please use your common sense when it comes to deciding whether or not to include a PS in your letter. You see, if you believe that every direct mail letter and every sales letter you write absolutely has to have a PS at the end of it, there is a danger that many readers will take one glance at your letter, observe the PS and say: *'Aha! this is only junk mail!'*.

Use the power of the PS with discretion, otherwise it may become a double-edged sword and have quite the opposite effect to what you intend.

SUMMARY OF CHAPTER 11:
HERE'S WHAT YOU SAY AND HOW YOU SAY IT

- ☐ The very first thing that readers look at when they open letters is the top left-hand corner where their name and address is. The next thing they read is the salutation. If you address them incorrectly in your sales letter, or spell their name wrongly, they will know immediately that you haven't a breeze who you are writing to.

- ☐ Some people don't like strangers addressing them by their first names, because they feel that this is an intrusion on their territorial space. Unless you know your reader, the best approach, and far and away the safest salutation approach, is to use the more formal opening: *Dear Mr. Murphy, Dear Ms. Smith,* etc.

- ☐ Try not to sign off your sales letter with a squiggle signature. A clear legible blue-ink signature conveys openness and honesty on the part of the writer.

- ☐ A PS at the bottom of your letter can be the second most important part of your sales letter. Use it wisely and remember, not every sales letter is strengthened by the use of a PS. If you plan to write to customers and potential customers on a regular basis, it makes good sense to use the PS sporadically ... otherwise your letters will look repetitious.

12. How Long Should Your Sales Letter Be?

> 'It isn't etiquette to cut anyone you've been introduced to. Remove the joint.'
> Lewis Carroll, *Through the Looking Glass* (1872), Ch.9.

How long should a good sales letter be? One page ... two pages ... maybe three or four pages or even more? What do you think?

When I ask this question, most people have no hesitation – no hesitation at all – informing me that a good sales letter must fit on a single A4 sheet of paper, otherwise nobody will read it.

This is not quite correct.

In fact, most research that has been carried out into the sales effectiveness of letters shows that sometimes, not always, a long letter can draw a better response than a shorter one. Some, indeed many of the most successful, direct mail copywriters insist on using long sales letters because they find that these always pull a better response for them.

But that's not to say that long sales letters will always attract a better response. It really depends on the product or service that you are selling and the skill of the copywriter at telling the story. I, for one, would much prefer to read a short interesting sales letter than a long rambling boring one.

But if you have an interesting story to tell, and you believe that you can write it all in an attention-grabbing way, then don't be afraid of spreading it out over more than one page. You see, if your sales pitch is really interesting, your readers will want to know all about it. And the more time that your readers are prepared to spend with you, the greater your chances of making a sale. Personally, I never go beyond two pages in a sales letter. That's because I believe that two pages gives you ample space to sell even the most complex product or service.

It's also because I firmly believe that the **appearance** of your sales letter is just as important as the words you use and the tone that you talk to your readers in. A sales letter that runs to three or more pages **looks** like too much hard work to read. So I've never written a sales letter of this size. But most of my most successful sales letters do run to two pages.

Part of the reason for this is because I like to use a very big type font in my sales letters. And when I use a large type font, I generally find that I need two pages to develop my sales pitch to my satisfaction. I will talk to you about the merits of using a large type font in my next chapter but the important message that I want to impart to you now is: *'Never be afraid to let your sales letter run over to a second page'*.

Now let me give you a little copywriter's tip on how to hold on to your readers' attention while they turn the page.

If you ever have a sales letter that takes up more than one page, you should always carefully end the last line of the first page in mid-sentence. This way, when your reader comes to the end of the first page, he/she will see that the sentences isn't finished so they will automatically turn to the next page to finish reading the sentence. By then, you've got them reading the top of the second page and they are well on their way to reading your entire two-page letter.

This 'end the page in mid sentence' strategy is widely used by professional direct mail copywriters. It's a simple little strategy for holding on to your reader's attention while they turn to the next page. Try it – it works!

One very interesting thing that I've learned over my many years of writing sales letters is that you don't always need a second sheet of paper to accommodate a two-page sales letter. In my experience, writing your sales letter on two sides of a single page seems to work just as well as writing it on a single side of two sheets of paper.

I really don't know why this is. Because, with the exception of a charity appeal letter, all logic tells me that two separate sheets of paper looks more impressive than a single sheet of paper written on both sides. The reason why I make charity appeal letters the exception is because using two sheets of paper to accommodate a two-page letter is definitely more expensive than writing on both sides of a single page, and charity supporters never like to see money being wasted.

Some of my clients wouldn't dream of sending out a sales letter to their customers and potential customers written on both sides of a single sheet of paper because it doesn't suit the image of their company or their business. And that's fine with me. But for those of you who are worried about the possible extra costs of sending out a two-page sales letter, my advice to you is to simply double-up on a single sheet of paper.

Here's another little tip that works well for me. I always find that if you put a little 'hand' symbol like this, at the bottom of the first page of a sales letter, it encourages the reader to continue reading. And you can further strengthen this, by writing a few encouraging words in small print beside the hand symbol.

Let me give you a few example of what I mean:

| Please read on and discover why you are our possible winner. | | I still haven't told you why we manufacture them in 'red' | |

SUMMARY OF CHAPTER 12:
HERE'S WHAT YOU SAY AND HOW YOU SAY IT

☐ Most research that has been carried out into the effectiveness of direct mail letters shows that a long sales letter can pull a better response than a short sales letter.

☐ If you have a good story to tell, and you believe that you can write it all in an interesting way, then don't be afraid of spreading it out over more than one page.

☐ Try not to go beyond two pages in a sales letter, however, because it will give the appearance of being too much hard work to read.

☐ If your sales letter runs to more than one page, a handy copywriter's tip is to always end your first page in mid-sentence. This will encourage your readers to turn automatically to the next page and finish reading the sentence.

☐ A little 'hand' symbol at the bottom of the first page will also encourage your readers to read on to the next page, especially if the hand symbol is supported by a small-print message reading something along the lines of:

> Turn over the page and I'll tell you
> why money is short-sighted.

13. MONEY IS SHORTSIGHTED!

I'll tell thee everything I can:
There's little to relate.
I saw an aged, aged man,
A-sitting on a gate.
Lewis Carroll, *Through the Looking Glass* (1872), Ch.8.

Let's say you are what I call 'a one-page letter person'. By this I mean, you like to restrict your sales letters to a single page. And you are in the process of writing an important sales letter but, despite your very best efforts, it runs two, three, four or five lines beyond the one page. What's the very first thing that most people in your situation do?

Take my word for it, the very first thing that most people do when they are faced with this problem is: **they reduce the size of the type font!** The font size is determined by the number of 'points' you select for your type – the greater the number of points, the larger the type and *visa versa*. For example:

... these words are printed in 10 point ...

... these words are printed in 18 point.

Since the chances are that you have written your draft letter in 12 point type, which is a common-enough type size for business letters, the very first thing that you'll do if your letter overruns the page is to reduce the type size down to 11 point or possibly 10 point.

A 10 point type size is very small – far too small for my liking -
- and, unless you're writing to teenagers who have excellent
eyesight, I would advise you not to go this small. So let's say you
compromise and instead you reduce it to 11 point – which is still
too small a font size for my liking. But, despite this reduction in
font size, you find that your sales letter still doesn't fit on the
single page. How are you going to overcome this problem
without resorting to using a 10 point type size?

Well, if you're like many people, the very next thing that you'll
do after reducing the font size is to adjust the margins at the side
of your letter. You make your margins smaller. This way, with
any luck at all, you'll be able to squeeze everything in to that all-
important one page! But c'mon! Be honest with yourself. What are
you left with?

Without hesitation, I'll say that you're left with a disgusting
looking small-print letter, which has mean margins! That's what
you're left with!

Believe me, your letter will look mean, off-putting and possibly
dangerous! Dangerous looking – because, all our lives, we've been
warned by our parents and our friends in the legal profession to
be careful of small print. Small print is what catches out good
people like you and me, when we discover to our horror that
things have gone frightfully wrong, and that we have no recourse
whatsoever because the vendor or service provider is legally
protected by what it says in the dreaded 'small print'.

Just about everything in a small print and mean-margin letter
is off-putting, paltry and stingy-looking. Add in a squiggle of a
signature at the end of it for good measure and you'll have in
your hands what I call 'a bad sales letter'. It's bad, because it looks
ugly. The reason I can say so confidently, and perhaps rudely,
these things to you is because I too have been there! In my early
copywriting days, I too used to hammer down the type size and
prise out the margins of my sales letters in my efforts to fit
everything on to a single page. Until, one day, quite by accident, I
discovered something very important.

As a result of my spending long hours bent over my computer,
there came a time in my life when I began to notice that, at the
end of a day's writing, I was suffering from headaches. Weeks
passed like this, until eventually I saw the writing on the wall, as
it were. And the writing on the wall clearly said to me 'go to your

optician and get your eyes checked'. So I did and, within a matter of days, my headache problem was solved. And in that one single visit to my optician, my entire written communications strategy changed ... for the better!

You see, what my optician gently explained to me was that, as naturally as night follows day, as each and every one of us gets older, our eyesight fades. For some people, this fading process occurs very gradually – so gradually that they don't even notice it happening. And, depending on what their occupation is, many people can happily live their lives without ever feeling the need to wear glasses.

By the time the majority of us reach our late-30s, however, if we don't already use glasses, it's wise at least to be alert to the fact that we may benefit from getting our eyes tested. Because, unbeknown to many of us, we could be straining ourselves unduly when we try to read small print and suchlike. It's possible – highly possible – that, in the beginning, we don't even notice that we are straining ourselves. It's just that we tire that little bit quicker when we are reading, with the result that it becomes more of an effort to concentrate for any length of time on written communications.

As it so happened, I was in my mid-40s when I visited the optician, and she told me that she wasn't really surprised to see me, as so many others like me arrive in her clinic to have their eyes tested around about my age or, as she rather pointedly said: *'They arrive much, much earlier!'*.

I explained to her how I spend my days reading and writing and she nodded wisely. *'You probably need glasses to help your reading'*, she said. But before she ushered me into the back clinic to test my eyesight thoroughly, she passed me a book – a bit like this book that you are now holding in your hands – and invited me to read a few lines of it. It was no great problem at all.

'Now, what I want you to do is to close your right eye, and to read a few lines of this book with your left eye only', she said. As luck would have it, I could read a few lines of the book without a bother. *'Next'*, she said, *'close your left eye and read me a few lines using your right eye only'*. I was absolutely astounded!

Because, for the first time ever, I realised that my right eye couldn't read a single word from a page in front of me. It was an eerie experience. Without thinking, still with my left eye closed, I moved the book further away from my face and, suddenly, with a huge sense of relief on my part, everything sprang into focus and I could happily read the print.

In simple layman's terms, what was happening was that, over the years, one of my eyes had become more pronouncedly long-focussed than the other. The upshot of this was that, gradually over time, I was doing all my reading with my good reading eye – my left eye. And since this eye was having to do double the job it was intended to do, it was getting tired much quicker and my 'easy-reading' concentration span was becoming shorter.

What astonished me about all of this was – and still does – I had never noticed it happening. Happily, in no time at all, I had a brand new pair of reading glasses and, like all the best happy-ending stories, *'I've lived happily ever after'*.

More practically, because I was now very conscious that, over time, everyone's eyesight fades naturally, I began to introduce a large 14 point Times New Roman type size into all my sales letters. My reason for doing this was that I wanted to be absolutely certain that everybody could read my sales letters without difficulty. This wasn't exactly a problem-free exercise, however.

The upshot of my decision to use a large type size was that the majority of my letters simply could not fit on to a single sheet of paper. So I ran them over onto the back of the page, or, if the client was unhappy about using the back of the page, onto a second page. All of this, of course, meant extra production costs for my clients which, in many cases they simply were not prepared to live with.

And okay, I didn't argue too strongly with my clients. Initially, in 95 out of a 100 cases, I simply edited the copy or reduced the type size to make it all fit comfortably on to a single page. But slowly, ever so slowly, some of my clients began to take an interest in what I was doing in the draft letters that I supplied to them. And within a very short period of time, some of the braver ones decided to test the response-pulling power of the larger type size. The reports and the results that came back were very favourable indeed.

Banks and financial institutions found that, when they mailed the over-50 age group with special offers in large easy-to-read 14 point type size, they got a better response that well and truly covered the additional paper costs involved of using a two-page letter. Charity clients of mine discovered the same thing. And soon the use of large type fonts began to gather momentum among my clients. Because it works! It really does.

Time and time again, I have found that large type pulls a better response. When you think about it, it makes sense, you know. So much so, that I coined the expression: *'Money is short-sighted!'*. And the minute I saw these words on the computer screen in front of me, I knew that what I was looking at was an important 'success-tip' for writing sales letters to the 40-plus age group.

Because it's a fact! *'... as you get older your eyesight fades naturally'*. Of course, the 'fading' process happens to some people earlier, but it's around about the 40 years of age mark that many people begin to notice that things ain't what they used to be in the eye-sight department. Other interesting things begin to click into place as you progress from this age.

What happens is an important combination of things. Things like, you are probably earning more money that you ever had before ... or will ever earn again! You see the sad truth of life is that most of us will have reached the zenith of our respective money-earning careers by the time we celebrate our 50th birthday.

Other exciting things happen as you move onward in age, like the mortgage is – at long last – becoming manageable. And the kids – at even longer last – are getting themselves jobs and coming off the family payroll.

And you are changing too! You see, by now, you've been around quite a bit. You've seen it all. You've done it all ... in fact, if you are not careful, you are in serious danger of becoming a VBP (a very bored person)

Aha! Imagine! You're a wealthy VBP ... with fading eyesight!

And some astonishingly good-looking 'pop chic' sends you a carefully-crafted sales letter typed up in a tiny, tiny, sans-serif typeface, which you just can't easily read!

C'mon! Be honest! What would you do if you were a well-off VBP with money burning a hole in your pocket, and you were faced with an unimportant-looking sales letter that was printed in a tiny typeface that you found difficult to read, or was printed in a pale, almost illegible, grey type that is very hard for you to focus on?

You'd junk it! That's what's you do!

That's why you have to be so careful with the size of the type you use in your sales letters. Keep in mind that not everybody is blessed with razor-sharp eyesight, particularly people in the 40+ age group. If you want to enrich the response-pulling powers of your sales letters, try using a larger type and talking big!

SUMMARY OF CHAPTER 13:
HERE'S WHAT YOU SAY AND HOW YOU SAY IT

☐ Sometimes letter writers resort to reducing the size of the type font to get everything on to one page. This can be counter-productive, especially if you are writing to a 40+ target group. Most people find it easier to read a larger type font size. Likewise, people who have literacy problems will find a larger type font more user-friendly.

☐ When space is tight, you might be tempted to narrow the margins of your letter. Don't do this. You'll end up with a letter that has mean margins. This gives the letter an ugly, mean and cheap appearance which, when coupled with a small type font, conveys the equivalent of unfriendly body language to the reader.

☐ Generally speaking, as people get older, in addition to their eyesight fading, they have more money to spend: *'Money is short-sighted!'.*

☐ This is a slogan that writers of charity appeal letters should keep carefully in mind because, time and time again, it has been shown that the most generous charity benefactors are those in the 40+ age group. It's also a slogan that many financial institutions could learn from, as investors in this age group represent a very sizeable proportion of the private investment market.

14. PARAGRAPH SPACING & JUSTIFYING

'No! No! Sentence first – verdict afterwards.'
Lewis Carroll, *Alice's Adventures in Wonderland* (1865), Ch.12.

Most people find it easier to read a larger type font size. However, the use of a large type font size in your sales letters is not without problems of its own.

The first, and most obvious, problem is that, if you type up everything in, let's say, a 14 point type size, the spaces between the paragraphs begin to look unduly large. They're out of harmony with the rest of your letter and, truth to tell, make your letter a somewhat lumpy looking read. Have a look at the couple of paragraphs below, and you'll see immediately what I mean:

This sentence, which is printed in 14pt Times New Roman, is very easy to read.

But the space between the paragraphs, which is also in 14pts, creates large wedges of 'white' that can reduce the visual impact of your message.

This becomes very obvious when you use short paragraphs.

And since most really good sales letters use a high number of short paragraphs and short sentences, there is a danger of too much 'white' appearing in your letter as a result of using a large type size.

If you are not careful, this will hinder rather than help your reader's concentration and when this happens ...

In the example above, the amount of 'white' space between the paragraphs has the effect of reducing the visual impact of the text. To stop this happening, it's wise to reduce the spaces between the paragraphs and minimise the visual impact of those white wedges. Look what happens when I reduce the paragraph spacing and, for added impact, indent one paragraph ever so slightly and make the word 'obvious' stand out in bold.

This sentence, which is printed in 14pt Times New Roman, is very easy to read.

But the space between the paragraphs, which is also in 14pts, creates large wedges of 'white' that can reduce the visual impact of your message.

This becomes very **obvious** when you use short paragraphs.

And since most really good direct mail letters use a high number of short paragraphs and short sentences there is a danger of too much 'white' appearing in your letter as a result of you using a large type size.

If you are not careful, this will hinder rather
than help your reader's concentration and
when this happens ...

Immediately, everything becomes easier on the eye to read. The
first thing that you should keep in mind when you use large type,
therefore, is you should reduce the amount of white space
between the paragraphs.

White spaces/gaps between your paragraphs have the effect of
reducing the amount of impact that the black printed text of your
copy has on your reader's eyes. The greater the amount of white
space on a page, the greyer your copy will look. And this is
exactly what you should try to avoid in your sales letters, because
vibrant black copy is easier, more impactful and faster to read
than slightly tired-looking grey copy.

Your computer wordprocessing package may automatically
keep the white paragraph spaces in proportion to the font size
that you are writing in. So, if you are using a 12-point font size,
your white paragraph space will be 12 points as well. If you are
using a 14-point size, the white paragraph space will be 14 points
and so on.

For maximum impact in a sales letter, I prefer to reduce my
paragraph spaces to approximately half the size of the actual font
size that I am using in my letters. Next time you are writing a
sales letter, try reducing the white spaces between your
paragraphs to approximately 50% of the font size that you are
using in your copy and see how different everything looks.
Immediately, your copy will look more prominent on the page.
You'll find that your eye will flow more easily from paragraph to
paragraph with the result that you'll read the entire letter much
faster.

And there's good news for 'one page' sales letter writers as
well! If you do this, not only will everything you write in your
sales letter look, and read, better, but with the extra space you
save by reducing the paragraph gaps, you'll probably be able to
fit in an extra line of sales copy into your page as well.

Now there's all kinds of ways that you can configure your
wordprocessing software to reduce the size of your paragraph
spacing, but I always use, what is for me, the easiest and most

straightforward way. I simply go through my draft sales letter and reduce the size of the paragraph spaces manually by pointing my cursor at the beginning of each paragraph space line, left-clicking on the mouse and, with my finger still pressed down, I slightly drag the mouse to the right. Then, once I lift my finger off the mouse, I'm left with a small solid black rectangular box on the screen in the white paragraph space line and I'm ready for business.

The next step is to go up to the font size box on the menu bar at the top of your screen and type in the font size that you'd like this blank white line to be. For example, if my sales letter is typed up in 14-point Times New Roman, I simply reduce the font size for the blank white line to 50% of 14 = 7 point. And I repeat this exercise for every white paragraph space in my letter. This may all sound a bit tedious but I think you'll be pleasantly surprised to find how little time it takes to complete it and to end up with a considerably enhanced-looking sales letter.

Try it, because, believe me, it's worth the little extra effort. Here's a little example of what happens when you reduce your paragraphs spacing to 50% of the font size that you are writing your sales letter in.

This is a three-sentence paragraph. This is the second sentence of the paragraph. I'm using a 14-point size Times New Roman font so my paragraph space will automatically be the same as the font size that I am using.

Wide 14pt ←—— paragraph space

This is a three-sentence paragraph. This is the second sentence of the paragraph. I'm using a 14-point size Times New Roman font.

Now turn the page and see the difference when I reduce the paragraph spacing by 50% to 7 point.

This is a three-sentence paragraph. This is the second sentence of the paragraph. I'm using a 14-point size Times New Roman font so my paragraph space will automatically be the same as the font size that I am using.

Closer 7pt paragraph space ◄

This is a three-sentence paragraph. This is the second sentence of the paragraph. I'm using a 14-point size Times New Roman font.

Often newspapers, magazines and newsletters don't use white paragraph spacing at all. Instead, they simply indent the first line of every paragraph after the first paragraph – they never indent the first paragraph. If you apply this technique to our example, this is how it will look.

This is a three-sentence paragraph. This is the second sentence of the paragraph. I'm using a 14-point size Times New Roman font so my paragraph space will automatically be the same as the font size that I am using.
    This is a three-sentence paragraph. This ◄ Indent
is the second sentence of the paragraph. I'm using a 14-point size Times New Roman font.

While this technique of indenting, without any white paragraph spacing, works very effectively in newspapers and magazines or anywhere that text is arranged in narrow columns, don't even think of using it in your sales letters. Because it will immediately make your very personal, one-to-one communication, sales letter look like an impersonal newspaper or magazine article.

Some sales letter copywriters like to use both techniques: white spaces between paragraphs, followed by an indented line of text at the beginning of the next paragraph. They argue that, if you start each clearly separated paragraph with an indented line, you draw the eye into the paragraph and encourage the reader to keep reading.

Whatever about the merits of this argument and I, for one, am certainly not going to dispute it. What I will say is that, if you indent the opening line of your paragraphs, you are, in my view, nudging your sales letter closer in appearance to an impersonal newspaper or magazine article format. And since this is exactly what I don't want to happen to my very personal sales letters, I never indent the opening paragraph lines of my sales letters.

There is a second little 'negative' that you should be aware of when you use a large type size. It is that, unless you are very careful, a large type size can create havoc with the appearance of sales letters that are typed up in 'justified' text.

WHAT IS JUSTIFIED TEXT?

Have a look at the two letters on the next page and see if you can work this one out for yourself. The first letter (Letter A) is totally 'justified', while the second letter (Letter B) is completely 'unjustified'. You'll note that each letter is written in 14 point Times New Roman font and that I've applied the 50% paragraph spacing principle outlined previously, so the paragraph spacing is seven points.

In both of the letters that follow, all the text is perfectly lined up on the left-hand margin but, in letter A, the text is **also** lined up on the right-hand margin. This is called 'justified' text.

In letter B, the text on the right-hand margin is not lined up, with the result that it has a rather ragged appearance on the right-hand margin. This is called 'unjustified' text.

In letter A, everything is lined up neatly and efficiently in military style on both margins, while in letter B the right-hand margin is irregular. Now let me ask you this question. Which sales letter do you think you can read faster and concentrate on more easily? Remember, I'm not asking you which looks more businesslike I'm asking you which one can be read faster.

Letter A: Justified

Dear Reader

I'd like to make you an offer that you simply cannot afford to ignore.

It's an opportunity for you – yes, you! – to become rich beyond your wildest dreams. And what's more, this offer comes to you with the absolute 100% guarantee of the World Bank.

Letter B: Unjustified

Dear Reader

I'd like to make you an offer that you simply cannot afford to ignore.

It's an opportunity for you – yes, you! – to become rich beyond your wildest dreams. And what's more, this offer comes to you with the absolute 100% guarantee of the World Bank.

The answer is 'unjustified letters'.

And the reason for this will become clear to you, if you have another look at letter A above. Look carefully and you'll see what the computer has done in order to achieve that line-up on the right-hand margin. It has varied the spaces between the words. In some cases, the gap between the words is larger than in others – sometimes irritatingly so. Take a quick look at that line *'It's an opportunity for you – yes, you! – to'* in letter A and you'll see immediately what I mean when I talk about irritating-looking spacing between words.

Now look again at letter B and you'll see that the reason why the right-hand margin is so ragged is because quite the opposite has happened. The computer has kept all the spaces between the words the same and the outcome is that the different lines of text have uneven endings on the right-hand margin.

The variable spaces that can occur between the words in justified text can have a very unsettling effect on the eyes. Sometimes, they can have a positively distracting effect on your reader and make it difficult for him or her to concentrate for any length of time on what is actually being said in the copy. And this is exactly what you don't want to happen to anyone who reads your sales letters.

As a general rule of thumb, the smaller the type size you use in your sales letter, the less you will notice the effects of justification. But, if you go up to a 14 point type size, which is what I am recommending to you on the basis that *'money is short-sighted'*, you'll notice the disjointed effect of justification immediately. A sales letter that is typed up in unjustified text is not only easier to read and to concentrate on, but also it's also more informal and user-friendly in appearance.

When you think about it, the more informal printed matter is in appearance, the more the printed message looks like somebody talking informally to you. And since a good sales letter effectively acts as a sales rep for your company, this more informal 'talking appearance' of unjustified text enhances the overall friendly sales tone of the message that your 'sales rep' is imparting to his or her readers.

If you find that you absolutely must use justified text in your letters for whatever reason, then my advice to you is that it's well worth your while to take a little bit of extra care working on your layout. Go over your draft letter carefully and by inserting an extra word here and breaking up a word there with a dash '–' at the end of a line, you should be able to smooth everything out and maintain the fast-flowing rhythm of your copy, **like I've done in this 7-line paragraph of carefully justified text.**

Most newspapers and books, by the way, are printed in justified text and are effortlessly easy to read. But this is because the publishers and printers have invested vast sums of money in technology, machines, editing and manpower expertise to ensure that the finished product is as near to perfect as they can make it.

It's people like you and I, who write sales letters with the help of common or ordinary computer wordprocessing programmes, who need to take great care that we don't produce 'justified' letters that are difficult to read and concentrate on. So, regardless of what size font you decide to use in your sales letter, my advice to you is to always opt for unjustified text. Yes! Even sales letters that use smaller point type look, and read, better with unjustified text.

SUMMARY OF CHAPTER 14:
HERE'S WHAT YOU SAY AND HOW YOU SAY IT

☐ Too much white space between the paragraphs of your letter tends to give it a grey appearance, which doesn't make the same impact on your readers' eyes as black text does.

☐ If you use a larger font, your wordprocessing programme may automatically make the space between the paragraphs larger, in proportion to the font size that you are using. This can give your letter a somewhat lumpy appearance. Try reducing the paragraph spaces manually to approximately 50% of the font size and this will immediately give your words more impact. And because you have linked your paragraphs more closely together, you also make your letter a faster read.

☐ Newspapers, magazines and newsletters often don't have any white space at all between the paragraphs; instead, they prefer to start each new paragraph after the opening paragraph with an indented line. Some direct mail letter copywriters do the same – they indent the opening line of each paragraph, in an effort to quickly draw the reader's eye into reading the paragraph. My advice to you is not to do this in your sales letters, as it makes them look like printed matter rather than personal communication. And personal communication is what a good sales letter is all about.

15. PARAGRAPH TRANSITIONS & CONNECTORS

> How cheerfully he seems to grin,
> How neatly spread his claws,
> And welcomes little fishes in
> With gently smiling jaws.
> Lewis Carroll, *Alice's Adventures in Wonderland* (1865), Ch.2.

Spaces between paragraphs are natural resting points for the reading eye. It's where your readers take a little breather, before moving on to the next paragraph. And it is for this reason that they can also be seen as danger zones from the writer's viewpoint. Because it's during these little pauses that many readers may decide that they have read enough of what you are telling them and that they don't want to read any further. So paragraph spaces are seepage holes, through which you can 'leak' readers.

By reducing the spaces between the paragraphs, you are working visually towards making that little breather as short as possible and, by making the 'leaking holes' smaller, you are actively encouraging your readers' eye to move effortlessly on to the next paragraph. But reduced spacing on its own is not enough to do the job effectively. You need to give your readers a few encouraging 'come along' words as well if you are to make the transition from one paragraph to the next as streamlined and as leakproof as possible.

These encouraging words are called 'paragraph connectors.'

Paragraph connectors help you to link your paragraphs together in your readers' mind and most direct mail copywriters take great pride in their ability to use them effectively. Public speakers and speechwriters are the real 'professionals' when it comes to using connectors, as they effortlessly move from one subject matter to another without losing their listeners' attention. And, if you listen carefully to a trained public speaker being interviewed on a television chat show, you'll notice that they leave no 'holes' in their flow of words and that, with a clever use of 'connectors', they always managed to convince the interviewer that what they are about to say is of far more interest that what they have already said.

Just when you think that they are coming to the end of making a point, or just when it looks as if the interviewer is about to change the subject, the trained speaker will quickly say something like:

◊   '... which brings me to my real point ...'

◊   '... but the most important thing of all is ...'

◊   '... so what I'm saying is ...'

◊   '... to sum up, therefore ...'

And once they use these 'connectors', they are off again and there's no stopping them.

Paragraph connectors work a dream in sales letters. They are deceptively easy to create. And the wonderful thing about them is that you can see the enhanced difference in your sales letters, the moment you start using them to make those paragraph gaps or 'holes' leakproof.

Let me give you two working examples of sales letters that have benefited from the use of connectors and then I'll share with you 200 of my own most popular paragraph connectors.

Letter 1

Dear Mr Hayes-McCoy

I'd like to introduce you to our new range of envelopes.

I'm enclosing a sample of each envelope in the range for your consideration and approval.

These are superior quality envelopes. They have been tried and tested on all the main brand envelope-inserting machines and they have passed the tests with flying colours.

Our prices are very competitive and provided we receive your order before 12 Noon we can guarantee you a next day delivery service to anywhere in the city.

I'm looking forward to the favour of your order.

Yours sincerely
Mark Jones
Sales Manager

Dear Mr Hayes-McCoy

I'd like to introduce you to our new range of envelopes.

 That's why I'm enclosing a sample of each envelope in the range for your consideration and approval.

As you can see, these are superior quality envelopes. They have been tried and tested on all the main brand envelope-inserting machines and they have passed the tests with flying colours.

I'd also like you to know that our prices are very competitive. **Furthermore,** provided we receive your order before 12 Noon we can guarantee you a next day delivery service to anywhere in the city.

I'm looking forward to the favour of your order.

Yours sincerely
Mark Jones
Sales Manager

Here's the original letter. And it's a regular enough letter as sales letters go.

Here's the same letter. I've added a few **'connectors'** and reduced the paragraph spacing to 50% of the font size to make those paragraph 'holes' as small as possible.

Letter 2

Dear Mr Hayes-McCoy

I wrote to you some time ago enclosing samples of our new envelope range.

I hope you have had an opportunity to feel the superior quality of these envelopes to see for yourself what excellent value they are for money.

Provided we receive an order before 12 Noon on a working day, we can guarantee you a 24-hour delivery service to anywhere in the city.

Our envelopes are used by many of Ireland's leading companies. We are looking forward to looking after all your future envelope requirements.

If you would like me to send you more samples, please don't hesitate to contact me.

Yours sincerely
Mark Jones
Sales Manager

Dear Mr Hayes-McCoy

You may recall that I wrote to you some time ago enclosing samples of our new envelope range.

Naturally, I hope you have had an opportunity to feel the superior quality of these envelopes to see for yourself what excellent value they are for money.

One of the big advantages that our company offers you is that provided we receive an order before 12 Noon on a working day, we can guarantee you a 24-hour delivery service to anywhere in the city.

As you may be aware, our envelopes are used by many of Ireland's leading companies. That's why we're looking forward to looking after all your future envelope requirements.

Needless to say, if you would like me to send you more samples, please don't hesitate to contact me.

Yours sincerely
Mark Jones
Sales Manager

Here's the original follow-up letter. And, again, it's a regular enough letter as sales letters go.

Here's the same letter. Again, I've added a few **'connectors'** and reduced the paragraph spacing to 50% of the font size for a faster flow.

Here's a list of 200 of my favourite paragraph connectors. Of course, this list of connectors is not all-inclusive. There are absolutely thousands of permutations and combinations of words that you can use to create very effective connectors for your own sales letters but you're welcome to use some of mine in your next sales letter if you wish.

200 PARAGRAPH TRANSITIONS & CONNECTORS

1	Actually …
2	After this, I simply must tell you that …
3	All things considered, I think that …
4	All this time, something important was …
5	All you need is …
6	And if you don't, then …
7	And now let me …
8	And then it happened …
9	And when he did, he …
10	And when it arrives, will you …
11	As the old saying goes, it's …
12	At first, I didn't know what to …
13	At the very least, it's …
14	At this stage, you're probably wondering if …
15	Be careful, because …
16	Because, if you do this for me, I'll …
17	Before I forget it, let me tell you that …
18	Before now, you had to …
19	Before this happens to you, you should …
20	Before we can, we …
21	Before we go any further, may I …
22	Before you even know it, you'll be …
23	Before you make your final decision, can I …
24	Believe me, if …
25	Best of all it's …
26	Bet you didn't see that …
27	Better still …
28	But do hurry because …

29   But those were the bad old days, now it is …

30   Choose carefully because …

31   Come with me while I introduce you to …

32   Customers often tell me that …

33   Do you know that …

34   Do you remember when …

35   Do you see that little …

36   Don't be fooled by …

37   Don't just take my word for it, let me show you …

38   Don't let anyone tell you that …

39   Don't stop reading just yet because …

40   Each time it happens, it's …

41   Even better, it's …

42   Eventually …

43   Every now and again, you …

44   Every time this occurs, it's …

45   Everyone is talking about it because …

46   First, let me assure you that …

47   For you, it definitely is…

48   Frankly, you will not get a better …

49   Furthermore …

50   Go on! It's …

51   Have a look at the enclosed and …

52   Have you ever been in …

53   Have you heard about …

54   Have you noticed that …

55   Hopefully, next time we …

56   However …

57   I almost forgot to mention that …

58   I do know one thing, which is …

59   I feel you should know that …

60   I immediately thought of you because …

61   I often forget to explain that …

62   I often wonder if …

63   I plan to …

64   I sometimes think that …

65   I want you to be the first to know that …

66   I've just remembered …

67	I've kept the best till last …
68	If it ever happens to you, will you …
69	If last night is anything to go by, then …
70	If this isn't enough, I'll …
71	If you asked me, I'd tell you that …
72	If you're anything like me, you'll …
73	If you're still not convinced, may I …
74	Immediately following this, it …
75	In no time at all you'll be …
76	In the interests of speed, I'll …
77	In the interests of saving you money, I'll …
78	Indeed it is, and …
79	Interestingly enough, it's …
80	It comes to you with …
81	It gets better as it goes on because …
82	It most definitely is …
83	It seems to me that …
84	It's a sickening thought because …
85	It's an offer which …
86	It's at this stage that most people ask …
87	It's even better because …
88	It's exciting to think that …
89	It's fair to say that …
90	It's good to know that …
91	It's great to see that …
92	It's guaranteed because …
93	It's not easy to be …
94	It's not everyone who …
95	It's not often that …
96	It's popular because …
97	It's something that we've been meaning to tell you …
98	It's the best that I've …
99	It's the feeling that …
100	It's the small things like this which …
101	It's welcome because …
102	Keep reading, because …
103	Last time this happened, we …
104	Last, but not least, …

105	Let me introduce you to …
106	Let me tell you why …
107	Let's move on and look at how …
108	Maybe it's because …
109	More and more satisfied customers are …
110	More importantly, …
111	More often than not, it's …
112	Moreover, …
113	Most amazingly, it …
114	Most peculiar, it's …
115	Never before has …
116	Never forget that …
117	Next, I must tell you how …
118	Nobody believed it because …
119	Nobody noticed that …
120	Nothing, absolutely nothing, will …
121	Now I can't be fairer that this, but …
122	Now I know you're not going to believe this, but …
123	Now let me tell you …
124	Nowadays, people want …
125	Observe how carefully …
126	Oddly enough, it's …
127	Of course it's for you and …
128	Of course, there's more …
129	Often what happens is …
130	Okay, but …
131	On reflection, I'd like you to …
132	Once …
133	Only once in my lifetime did …
134	Only yesterday, it …
135	People sometimes tell me that …
136	Perhaps the most important thing is …
137	Permit me to …
138	Picture this …
139	Plus there's a …
140	Read it carefully because …
141	Read on and …
142	Reading between the lines, it was …

143   Regrettably …

144   Sadly …

145   Seldom, if ever, it …

146   Sometimes it's …

147   Stop a moment and consider this …

148   Strangely, …

149   Successful people often say that …

150   Take great care with …

151   Take your time because …

152   Tell me! Have you ever …

153   That was the moment it became …

154   That's because you …

155   That's not all …

156   That's right, it's …

157   That's the reason why …

158   The best thing about it is …

159   The fascinating thing is …

160   The first time I tried it, I was …

161   The good news is that …

162   The important message is …

163   The interesting development is that …

164   The only explanation for this is …

165   The reason why it's excellent value is …

166   The reason why you have been selected is …

167   The remarkable thing is …

168   The truth is that …

169   The upshot of it all is …

170   The wonder of it is …

171   There comes a time when …

172   There's more, of course there's more, …

173   There's no way that …

174   Therefore, …

175   They sure do, and …

176   This is important because …

177   To get the best bargain, you must …

178   To sum it up for you in five words, …

179   Try it yourself and ….

180   Up to now, it …

181   Very quickly, let me explain what ...

182   Very soon, it will be ...

183   Well done! You've ...

184   What I mean is ...

185   What makes it stand out is ...

186   What will interest you most is ...

187   What's more, there's ...

188   Whatever you do, don't leave it ...

189   When did you last have ...

190   When I say that it's ...

191   When it arrived, it was ...

192   When this happens, it's ...

193   When we meet, I'll ...

194   Will you do this immediately because ...

195   You are going to enjoy the next bit because ...

196   You may recall that ...

197   You stand to gain most if ...

198   You'll find this hard to beat ...

199   You're absolutely right because ...

200   Zone in on your favourite colour quickly because ...
        (OK, I had to have one that started with 'Z'.)

SUMMARY OF CHAPTER 15:
HERE'S WHAT YOU SAY AND HOW YOU SAY IT

☐ Long paragraphs look off-putting, particularly in sales letters. So you should always keep your paragraphs short. Avoid going beyond six lines of text in any paragraph.

☐ However, when you use a high number of short paragraphs, you inevitably end up with a higher number of white paragraph spaces, or holes in your text. These holes are danger zones because you can 'leak' readers through them.

☐ That's why it makes sense to make these holes (or paragraph spaces) appear as small as possible, so that the readers' eyes will skip quickly over them into the next paragraph.

☐ By using connectors to start paragraphs, you help your readers' minds, as well as their eyes, to skip over into the next paragraph and keep reading.

☐ In a nutshell, you make the paragraph spaces more leakproof, with the result that you leak fewer readers. That increases the chance of your entire letter being read by more of your readers.

16. IMPROVING YOUR WRITING STYLE

'When I use a word', Humpty Dumpty said in a rather scornful tone, 'it means just what I choose it to mean – neither more nor less. The question is,' said Humpty Dumpty, 'which is to be master – that's all'.
Lewis Carroll, *Through the Looking-glass* (1872), Ch.6.

There's a wonderful quotation from the novelist, Alexander Pope (1688 - 1748), that says:

> *Words are like leaves, and where they abound,*
> *Much fruit of sense beneath is rarely found.*

It's called verbiage! I often find that when people are not sure about what they are writing about, they tend to use woolly words or they bury their message under a mountain of words. Some writers are actually very good at this and you can find yourself reading something that looks and sounds very important but, often, by the time you've finished reading it, when you get down to brass tacks, you are not quite sure what the writer is saying. As Pope says: '... *much fruit of sense beneath is rarely found'*.

If you want some learned advice about the skill of creating a good written communications' style, let's go back two-and-a-half thousand years and listen to the words of one of the wisest communicators of all. I'll tell you who he is in a few moments. First, let's look at what he said.

'Style,' he said, *'to be good must be clear. Clearness is secured by using words that are current and ordinary'.*

Some writers appear to have a horror of using *'current and ordinary'* words and deliberately set out to impress their readers by using uncommon, obscure words. If you use unusual words, jargon or technical terms, your reader may simply not understand what you are saying. Even worse, you may end up conveying a message that is quite the opposite of what you intended to say.

For example, if I were to write you a sales letter inviting you to come to one of the most memorable Atlantic coast seaside towns in Ireland – a place that always reminds me of *'the halcyon days of my youth'*, what exactly am I referring to when I use that lovely sounding, but seldom heard, word: *'halcyon?'.*

Am I talking about my wild days of devilish debauchery and hectic holiday living, or am I fondly remembering those calm tranquil days when life beside the sea was easy and everything was smooth and slow?

Many people think that *'halcyon days'* refer to furiously fast living and enterprising energetic times when, in fact, *'halcyon'* means quite the opposite. It means calm, peaceful, serene days and the word is derived from the tranquillity of the Pacific, rather than the Atlantic, ocean. Keep in mind the words of our wise communicator: *'Clearness is (best) secured by using words that are current and ordinary'.*

Now let's hear what he says next.

WRITE THE WAY YOU SPEAK

'You must disguise your art', he advises us, *'and give the impression of speaking naturally and not artificially'.*

Yes! Effectively what our wise communicator is telling us is to 'write the way you speak'. But look what he says next: *'Strange words and invented ones must be used sparingly and on few occasions'.*

Two and a half thousand years ago, they had the same problem that we have today. Then, people were using obscure words and making up words of their own in the hope of impressing their listeners and readers, just like so many companies and business executives of today.

Of course, I love playing with words – rich-sounding words, provocative words, unusual words, and sensual words. And I indulge myself in taking the time to seek out words that best capture the description of an image or an atmosphere that I want to share with my reader. But I control such indulgences when I am writing an important sales letter.

That's because I know that I will get the best response if my readers understand every single word that I use. It's part of the skill of writing a really great sales letter. It's the skill of being able to create a very persuasive sales message using ordinary, everyday, words that everybody understands.

'The aptness of your language is one thing that makes people believe in the truth of your story', says our wise communicator.

I love that last bit. Remember, crisp clear writing is more believable than wondrous woolly words, every time! Why is this? Let's see what our wise communicator says:

'Their (your readers') *minds are drawn to the false conclusion that you are to be trusted from the facts that you seem to be talking to them'*.

He's not exactly sparing any punches here, is he? He's telling you straight out that you can hoodwink your readers into believing just about anything if you give it to them straight, using simple, ordinary, apt words. Now I'm not suggesting, not for one moment, that you try and hoodwink your readers into believing something that is blatantly untrue, but I *am* drawing your attention to the strong, persuasive, selling powers of using plain language in all your sales letters.

Let me give you these wise words altogether so that you can see what Aristotle is telling us about how to create a good communication style. Because it is none other than Aristotle in *The Rhetoric* who says:

Style to be good must be clear. Clearness is secured by using words that are current and ordinary. You must disguise your art and give the impression of speaking naturally and not artificially. Strange words and invented ones must be used sparingly and on few occasions. The aptness of your language is one thing that makes people believe in the truth of your story. Their minds are drawn to the false conclusion that you are to be trusted from the facts that you seem to be talking to them.

Aristotle, *The Rhetoric*

Mind you, if you want to hear a more modern voice telling you how to develop your writing style, all you have to do is look at what 'Papa' Hemingway says about good writing:

> 'The most essential gift for good writing is a built-in shock-proof shit detector.'

I always like the way Hemingway calls a spade a spade. But let me do a quick flash back to Alexander Pope, who also tells us that:

> 'True ease in writing comes from art, not chance,
> As those move easiest who have learn'd to dance.'

Here, Pope is warning us not to expect instant successful results. It takes time, sometimes far longer than you might expect, to write a really good sales letter.

HOW LONG ... ?

I write sales letters for my living. I've been doing it for years, and I like to think that I write them better than most. On average, it takes me three solid hours' work to write a letter that I am satisfied with.

Sometimes clients look at me in amazement and say, in effect, 'Come off it, McCoy, surely you didn't spend three hours writing this very straightforward letter?' And because my fees are based on my time input, I'm often at the receiving end of comments about padding my fees and suchlike. But it's true!

Hey! No! It's not true that I pad my fees; it's true that it takes me three hours on average to write a really good sales letter.

Quite often, when I am working on a sales letter, I will have a rough draft of it completed in no time at all. Then the hard work starts. I will spend hours going over and over my draft letter, time and time again. I will do a little edit here. I will take a word out there. I will rearrange the order of my paragraphs. I will go away and do something else and come back later with a fresh pair of eyes and a new mind-frame and look at my draft letter again.

Often – too often for my liking – I will tear up the page and start again. Now and again, I amaze myself by finding that, after all the changes I've made, I end up back where I started. And, give or take a few commas, the letter that I am finally satisfied with, is little different to the very first draft that I had typed up three hours previously.

Never be afraid to tear everything up and start afresh. This is not even half as destructive as it sounds. You see, your mind has already done all the hard work accumulating information and deciding what you want to say. And a fresh start is sometimes a far quicker way of producing a really good sales letter than spending hours trying to knock a badly-structured draft letter into shape.

Oscar Wilde had somewhat similar experiences with editing his writing. At the beginning of the last century, he is reported to have announced:

'I was working on the proof of one of my poems all the morning, and took out a comma. In the afternoon, I put it back in again.'

One can't help smiling at the sheer exuberance – possibly arrogance – of anyone who could make such a pronouncement. But if it were true, and very possibly it is true, just think about that precious comma that Oscar Wilde put back in again.

That comma is probably still with us today, as generation after generation of Wilde fans continue to get endless pleasure and enjoyment from reading his works. Now I'm not for one moment going to suggest that your really great sales letter is going to survive the tests of time, but one of the reasons why Wilde's work is still so universally acclaimed is because he spent so much time getting it right.

If you want to write a very persuasive sales letter, you should be prepared to invest whatever extra time it takes to make absolutely sure that you get it right for your company or your product. **And get it right for your readers too!**

Remember that the true worth of a sales letter is measured in the response it generates from its readers. So, when you are investing your time in getting your sales letter right, you should always give some thought to how your readers are going to respond to your letter.

HOW READERS RESPOND

Some companies have very clear target groups for their products or services. For example, one of my clients sells only to building contractors. And, quite often, will address his sales letters to them on-site. He knows from experience that, the clearer his writing style, the better the response he will get because most of his readers will read his sales letter 'on the move', as it were.

As part of this simple clarity approach, he gives them a telephone number to respond to and he always ends his sales letters with an invitation to *'call me now!'* You see, he knows that not every builder will have pen, paper and an envelope on site to complete and post an order form, but nowadays no builder goes anywhere without his mobile phone.

Another client targets 'creatives' in advertising companies and he knows from experience that what stimulates them is clever headlines and an up-beat copy style with a decidedly humorous approach. He finds that, quite often, with this particular target group, he can play on words and even (dare I say it) use makey-up words, and they love it.

But then again, I have another client who has learned from bitter experience that a humorous copy style simply doesn't pay. And no! He doesn't work in the financial services sector, where humorous copy is always a risky thing to use; he runs a chain of household goods stores. He finds that warm, simple, considerate copy pulls the best response for him every time.

Charity clients of mine find that the keynote for success is sincerity. A simple, sincere, uplifting appeal for help, using plain words, and carefully telling the readers exactly what is required from them, almost always works better than a gloom-and-doom or shock-treatment style approach.

Clients who write to accountants tell me that these professional people enjoy detail. So, if you adopt a copy style that allows the detail to speak for itself, your chances of convincing them to buy your products or services are greatly enhanced.

But life, I'm afraid is never this simple. Most companies sell their products and services to several different target groups. Take an airline, for example. They sell seats to just about everybody. Take a large department store. They sell to just about everybody too. Or take a swimming pool or a fitness centre. They sell to people of all ages, shapes and sizes.

Over the years, I have discovered that the copy style that works best for 'everybody' is an easy-flowing warm friendly helpful style that:

◊ Is not too clever

◊ Is not too smart

◊ Is not too complex

◊ Takes the time to spell out the benefits of the product or service being sold and answers the WI-IFM (*What's in it for me?*) question for the readers

◊ Above all, has a high 'U-count'.

This is a simple copy approach to describe but it's a very difficult style of copy to get right at the first attempt. It takes time. It may take you up to 10 different draft attempts to achieve. But the final product is worth every minute you invest in it, if you end up with a sales letter that:

◊ Is easy to read aloud

◊ Sounds like somebody is talking to you

◊ Is easy on the eye

◊ Clearly tells you how you can obtain the product or service being offered.

SUMMARY OF CHAPTER 16:
HERE'S WHAT YOU SAY AND HOW YOU SAY IT.

☐ A good sales letter is like good whiskey, it takes time to perfect. So take your time!

☐ Remember, the aptness of the language you use makes your readers believe in the truth of what you are saying to them.

☐ Never be afraid to tear everything up and start afresh. This is not even half as destructive as it sounds. You see, your mind has already done all the hard work accumulating information and deciding what you want to say. And a fresh start is sometimes a far quicker way of producing a really good sales letter than spending hours trying to knock a badly-structured draft letter into shape.

☐ The copy style that works best for 'everybody' is an easy-flowing warm friendly helpful style that:

◊ Is not too clever

◊ Is not too smart

◊ Is not too complex

◊ Takes the time to spell out the benefits of the product or service being sold and answers the WI-IFM (*What's in it for me?)* question for the readers.

◊ Above all, has a high 'U-count'.

17. STRUCTURING YOUR SUCCESSFUL SALES LETTER

> 'The time has come', the Walrus said,
> 'To talk of many things;
> Of shoes ... and ships ... and sealing wax
> Of cabbages ... and kings ...
> And why the sea is boiling hot ...
> And whether pigs have wings.'
> Lewis Carroll, *Through the Looking Glass* (1872), Ch.4.

I've always been enchanted by Lewis Carroll's wise old Walrus who walked along a sandy beach, *'close at hand'* with the Carpenter and wondered *'if seven maids with seven mops swept it for half a year'*, could they ever successfully clear away all the individual little grains of sand. *"'I doubt it said the Carpenter', and shed a bitter tear."*

AIDA

Now what I want to tell you is how to bring together, with the help of the mysterious Lady AIDA, all those little grains of wisdom that I have shared with you so far.

There is a universal formula – a very easy formula to use – that has helped direct mail copywriters all over the world to structure their all-important sales letters, brochures and adverts to achieve maximum impact and maximum results.

This formula is known as the 'AIDA' formula. Some direct marketing copywriters prefer to work to a slightly larger version called the AIDCA formula, but I've always found that the simpler Lady AIDA works best for me.

What AIDA stands for is:

◊   **A = ATTENTION:** Simply put, what this means is that you should always start your very persuasive sales letter by capturing your readers' attention. Your headline, your opening words, your starting sentence or your very first paragraph should be structured in such a way that your readers' attention is immediately captured and he or she is drawn, out of curiosity, into reading your letter.

◊   **I = INTEREST:** Once you have your readers' attention, you now need to hold on to them so that they read the rest of your letter. You need to hold their interest.

◊   **D = DESIRE:** At this stage, you've successfully captured your readers' attention and you've carefully held their interest. Now you must create a desire in their minds to do what you want them to do. For example: to buy something, to contact you, to prepare themselves to be contacted by you, to agree to meet you or whatever.

◊   **A = ACTION:** The final step is to tell your readers exactly what action you want them to take the moment they finish reading your sales letter. It's exactly like a sales rep closing a sale.

AIDA = Attention, Interest, Desire and Action! There you have it! There is the formula that so many professional writers use to bring them success in their sales letters. By the way, that extra 'C' in the more extended AIDCA formula, which I referred to at the start of this chapter, stands for 'Conviction'.

Some copywriters prefer to structure their letters as follows: Attention, Interest, Desire, Conviction and Action. Personally, I don't see the need for the extra 'C for Conviction' in the formula because, if you press the Interest and Desire buttons with enough conviction, everything else should fall neatly into place.

Hey! This is good going, isn't it? You've now got a well-tested and proven international formula for success on how to structure your very persuasive sales letter. All you have to do is apply it and you are well on your way along the highway to becoming rich beyond your wildest dreams. Simple, isn't it!

No! It's not that simple. At least, I didn't find it at all simple when I was first introduced to the success-promising powers of awesome Lady AIDA. Okay, as formulae go, it's a nice simple sounding one. It looks good, and it certainly sounds authoritative. But it left me with a serious want: I wanted to know how exactly do you use it? For example: how on earth do you get **attention** in a sales letter? For that matter, how do you get **interest**?

How Does the AIDA Formula Work?

In my search for the answer to this question, I began to keep a weather-eye open for AIDA every time I picked up a book or an article on direct marketing or writing successful sales letters. I learned one thing from this exercise and I deduced another important piece of information.

What I learned is that it's amazing how universal the AIDA formula is. Just about every good book on direct marketing and direct mail has a reference to the AIDA, or the AIDCA, formula somewhere in it. Some even have entire chapters or sizeable segments of the book devoted to AIDA. All proudly presented the formula to me and told me exactly what each letter in AIDA (or AIDCA) stood for. Without exception, they assured me that this was a useful formula to follow, but none that I read told me how exactly I could apply it.

What I deducted from all this was that maybe – just maybe – many of the authors of these books and publications simply hadn't a breeze how AIDA actually worked in practice. Or if they did, they either didn't want to share this information with me or they didn't feel that it was necessary to explain to me how AIDA actually works. Huh!

Well, let *me* put AIDA into action for you.

In a few moments, I am going to make you a very special offer and I'm going to immediately follow this up by asking you an important question. What I want you to do then is to pause for a moment and to answer my question honestly to yourself. Okay, here's the offer.

'Because you are a reader of my book, I want to do something very special for you. I want to give you one million Euro! Yes! I want you to have one million Euro!'

Now, my important question to you is: do you believe me? Do you believe that I want to give you, my anonymous reader, one million euro?

Of course you don't. Sure, it would be nice to get one million Euro by simply reading this book, but you and I know that life isn't like this and that an opportunity to get a million Euro doesn't exactly come our way too often. So your honest answer to my question is a big *'NO, I don't believe that you want to give me a million Euro'*.

Now read the following message very carefully because it could have something very special in it for you.

Dear Reader of my book

I'd like to give you a million Euro. I really would. What's more, I'd love to give it to you on your next birthday at exactly 10 o'clock in the morning.

What I'm planning to do is stand outside your local post office (the one down the way from you) at 10am on your birthday with a million Euro in my briefcase. And if you hand me this page of my book, as proof of who you are, I'll be delighted to give you your very special €1m birthday present.

To make it easy for you to recognise me, I'll hold a copy of this book in my left hand and I'll have your million Euro in my brown – not black – briefcase in my right hand. The reason why I'm using my brown briefcase is because it has a handy little zip at the bottom of it, which allows you to expand the entire middle section of the briefcase if you need to put a lot into it.

And believe me, I'll need all the space I can get. Because have you ever seen a million Euro in crisp new 20 Euro notes? It takes up a lot of space. There's another thing too. It's actually very heavy. But, of course, it's all yours.

Now, I do have one little stipulation, I'm afraid. You see, have you ever stood outside your local post office at 10am in the morning with a million Euro in crisp 20 Euro notes in an expandable brown brief case? No! Well let me tell you, it's not very safe! Anyone can mug you.

So I'm only going to wait for you for five minutes ... not a minute more. At exactly 10.05am, if you don't turn up, I'm going to leave. And I'm going to go to the next post office where I've already invited somebody else to meet me at 10.30am that morning.

By the way, the reason why I want you to have first option on that million Euro is because I really do like you.

I'll see you outside your local post office at 10am on your birthday. Make sure you keep the time free. In fact, why not mark the appointment in your diary now, while the time, '10am', is still fresh in your mind.

Kindest personal regards

Robert

That was fun, wasn't it? Now imagine, just imagine, if it were true? The fascinating thing about this offer, and I'm willing to bet you a king-size *Mars* bar on this, is that I know it will work, in fact I'm absolutely certain about this. I'm certain that, if I had the names and addresses of all my readers, plus a few basic details like the date of your birthday, the name of your local post office, what it looks like, what's the colour of its front door and maybe one or two details about the street in which it is located ... **I could get most of you to turn up!**

Yes! I genuinely believe this. I believe that, if I had the appropriate personal details, I could write an individual letter to each and every one of my readers and get far and away the majority of you to turn up outside your local post office, or nearby hotel, at exactly 10am on the morning of your next birthday.

But, and wait for it! I could get most of you to turn up ... **on the other side of the road!**

Why on earth would you be on the other side of the road?

The answer to this question is simple. It's because you wouldn't want to make a fool of yourself. That's why!

You see, if you got a sufficiently persuasive letter from me, complete with appropriate details like: *'Congratulations, my publisher has just told me that you are the one millionth person to buy my book and I'd like to mark the occasion in a very special way'.*

The very first thought that would probably go through your mind is that this can't possibly be for real. This must be a joke! But, if I do my copywriting job properly, I should, at the very least, be able to plant a seed of doubt in your mind – a seed of doubt that makes your mind ask yourself questions like this:

'What if it is actually for real? Maybe I am the 1,000,000th person to read his book. Maybe this guy really has a million Euro to give away? Maybe he's a nice nut!'.

It certainly would be worth your while just to turn up and check it out, wouldn't it? After all, you could probably find some other good reason to pass by your local post office at 10am that morning. So it wouldn't be a total waste of your time. You could always do a bit of shopping, couldn't you? Problem is that I just might be playing a practical joke on you. In which case, you'd look a wee bit foolish standing outside the post office at 10am waiting for me to turn up, wouldn't you? But what if ... what if ...! It could be worth a million Euro to you.

So, if you're anything like me, what you'd do is play safe. Turn up on the other side of the road, or park your car in a handy place where you can observe the front of the post office without anybody observing you. This way, you get the best of all worlds. Because, if I turn up, as promised, with my battered brown briefcase you can come over and say *'Hi Robert! I'm here to collect my million Euro'*.

And if I don't turn up, you can go quietly go about your business, do some shopping or whatever **and nobody will ever know!** You'll not have made a fool of yourself in anybody's eyes. How's that! Actually, this is the way most people think and it's probably what most people would do. There's a name for this behaviour in direct marketing. It's called *'fear of loss'*.

FEAR OF LOSS

There's a practical direct marketing definition, which goes:

'... fear of loss is a far more powerful sales tool than hope of gain.'

By this I mean, if you tell me exactly what I will lose by not following a prescribed course of action, I will pay more attention to you than if you simply offer me a promise of gain.

In the above scenario what you stand to lose if you fail to turn up is one million Euro. And hey! If you don't turn up that million Euro – *your* million Euro! – in all probability, will go to the person who is already invited to turn up at 10.30am that morning outside the post office down the road.

Hmmm! It doesn't cost you much to turn up does it? And let me remind you again that, if you don't turn up, that guy down the road could be laughing all the way to the bank with *your* million Euro.

Okay! Time to stop dreaming. Let's go back and examine that letter again and see exactly how the AIDA formula is applied to it.

A = ATTENTION

You must open your letter by capturing your reader's attention. The question is how do you get attention? The simple, straightforward, answer to this question is: The best way for you to get attention in the opening paragraph of your sales letters is to use one of those magic words that I introduced you to in **Chapters 2** and **3** of this book.

Here they are again:

◊   Win ...

◊   Guarantee ...

◊   Breakthrough ...

◊   Save ...

◊   How to ...

◊   Free ...

◊   New ...

◊   Now ...

◊   At last ...

◊   and there's the platinum word: You.

Remember, I mentioned to you that these words are the hidden persuaders. These are the "goodness and greedy" words. These are the words that your readers will hear on the WI-IFM 24-hour radio. These are the words that have been tested time and time again and they work! Do you recall my telling you that the platinum magic word 'You' is the most important word of all? So if you want to capture your readers' attention you should try, if at all possible, to use a magic word in your opening paragraph.

As you can see, I've deliberately opened my letter using no less than three platinum magic words 'you' (including one 'your') in the opening paragraph of my very special offer to you.

> I'd like to give you a Million Euro. I really would. What's more, I'd love to give it to you on your next birthday at exactly 10 o'clock in the morning.

Effectively, what I'm doing here in my first paragraph is using the magic word 'You' three times with the objective of capturing your attention. Did I succeed? I think that I did, I think that most people would pay attention – even if only for a few seconds – to a letter addressed to them with an opening paragraph like this. To get attention, therefore, you should always try and use a magic word in the opening paragraph of your sales letter.

Here are a dozen samples of opening paragraphs where I've applied the magic word technique to try and capture attention. To make it easy for you to see at a glance where I'm using the magic words, I've underlined each one of them. Have a look at these examples and judge for yourself whether I have successfully accomplished my task.

1.	2.	3.
Dear reader	Dear reader	Dear reader
I'll never forget the first time I saw her! **You** can't imagine how wonderful she looked. Absolutely stunning! But do **you** know that…	I sang it! And I'm sure that at some stage in **your** life **you've** sung this song too! But have **you** ever noticed how every time **you** hear the words **you** …	This is a letter that I find very difficult to write. **You** see, I don't know **how to** start. But it's getting late **now**, so I'm going to try one more time to see if I can accurately describe to **you** what I saw.

4.
Dear reader

Have **you** any idea what it's like to be blind? Well, I'd like **you** to take the very large envelope that this letter comes to **you** in and carefully pull it over **your** head …

5.
Dear reader

It happened to me not so very long ago. I certainly wouldn't like it to happen to **you**. That's why I'm writing to tell **you** about it.

6.
Dear reader

Now I know **you** are going to find this very hard to believe. But it's true! What's more, for **you**, it's absolutely **Free**!

7.
Dear reader

At last, the evenings are getting longer. And while we can't **guarantee** that we won't experience another cold spell, there is one sure thing that I'd like **you** to know about immediately.

8.
Dear reader

A very odd thing happened to me on my last birthday. It was a completely **new** experience for me and my family – an experience that I'd **now** like to share with **you**.

9.
Dear reader

This is a letter that could **save** somebody's life. But before I tell **you** about the remarkable **new breakthrough** that has happened in the field of medical science, let me show **you how to** ...

10.
Dear reader

Next week, we're having a SALE in our store! But it's a sale with a difference. It's different because it's by invitation only. And this letter is **your** personal invitation.

11.
Dear reader

Have **you** ever noticed how all pension investment opportunities look very much the same? But not every pension plan offers **you** a **guarantee** like this...

12.
Dear reader

I've got some good news for **you**. In fact, if **you'd** like to take advantage of it **now**, I can **guarantee you** that **you** will never have to worry about noisy neighbours again.

Each of the openings above makes good use of the magic words, particularly the platinum magic word to try and capture your attention. Each of the above opening paragraphs sets out to do something else too! It sets out to capture your attention and make you want to **read more**.

For example, what is it that can guarantee you that you'll never have to worry about noisy neighbours again? What happened that is so difficult to describe? And why is this letter so difficult to write? What was the odd experience that happened to me on my last birthday? Which song am I talking about?

All of these are unanswered questions, interesting questions, and the only way the reader is going to learn the answer to them is to read on! Most people will be curious enough to read more. I've deliberately structured these openings to make it as difficult as possible for the average reader to tear up the letter without reading any further.

In short, I've achieved what I set out to do; I've captured my readers' attention. Now, my next job is to hold on to this attention for as long as possible – at least, until the end of my next paragraph and, hopefully, until the very end of my letter. So I'm going to immediately apply the next part of the AIDA formula which is I = Interest.

I = INTEREST

The question is: how do I hold on to my readers' interest?

If you go back and have a quick look at my *'million Euro on your birthday'* letter, you'll see that, in my second paragraph, I immediately start getting into detail about how, where and when I plan to give you *your* money.

> What I'm planning to do is stand outside your local post office (the one down the way from you) at 10am on your birthday with a million Euro in my briefcase. And if you hand me this page of my book, as proof of who you are, I'll be delighted to give you your very special million Euro birthday present.

It's the detail that makes things interesting. Detail, detail and even more details! What's happening here is that, the more details I give you, the more believable my offer sounds. You'll notice also that I continue giving you details in my third paragraph.

> To make it easy for you to recognise me, I'll hold a copy of this book in my left hand and I'll have your million Euro in my brown – not black – briefcase in my right hand. The reason why I'm using my brown briefcase is because it has a handy little zip at the bottom of it, which allows you to expand the entire middle section of the briefcase if you need to put a lot into it.

I talk about things like holding a copy of this book in my left hand. I tell you that I'll have your million Euro in my brown briefcase, not my black one. I share an interesting little bit of information with you about how my brown briefcase has a handy little zip at the bottom of it. All of these little details are interesting, but they really don't answer the paramount question in your mind. The question, of course is: *'Why me?'*.

If you tear up my letter at the end of the third paragraph, you'll never know the answer to this question. In fact, the only way you are going to learn the answer to this question is to read on. What I'm working on very hard here is to get you to keep reading – **holding your interest**. Because the more you read, and the longer I can hold on to your attention, the more I increase my chances of selling you on the idea that I really do want to give you a million pounds.

The interest is in the detail and the detail should come in the I = Interest part of your letter. Remember, the I = Interest part of your letter **follows immediately** after the A = Attention opening part of your letter.

This is very important for you to know. Because far too many writers of sales letters get confused about this, with the result that they either leave out the interesting details entirely or – big big big No NO! – they present the details in the wrong place.

Let me quickly explain to you what I mean by 'presenting the details in the wrong place'.

How many times have you read a sales letter that opens something like this?

Dear Mr Hayes-McCoy

As one of the largest printers in the country operating out of our new 10,000 sq. mts. state-of-the-art premises, which is located just beside the airport, we can offer you a leading edge in modern technology. We employ 200 people working on a 24-hour basis to ensure JIT delivery. With our nation-wide fleet of 20 delivery trucks and vans no job is too big or too small for us. For really large orders, we use a ZP1067A rapid duplex printing configuration, which has an astonishingly fast throughput capacity of ... and so on and so forth.

Okay, I know that I'm probably exaggerating and laying it on a bit heavy and cumbersome in the above example but do you see the point I'm making?

The point I'm making is that all of this detail is in the wrong place. It shouldn't be in the opening paragraph. Detail = Interest, and interest in the AIDA formula comes after A = Attention. If you apply the AIDA formula to the above letter you end up with a structure, which reads something like this:

Dear Mr Hayes McCoy

No matter how large, or how small, your printing requirements are, I believe that we can save you a considerable amount of money.

The reason why I am so confident about this is because we are one of the largest printers in the country operating out of our new 10,000 sq. Mts. state-of-the-art premises which is located just beside the airport ... and so on and so forth.

Do you see what I have done? I've simply introduced an A = Interest paragraph at the beginning of the letter. I've used the magic words 'your', 'you' and 'save' in my new opening paragraph. Plus, I have answered the reader's WI-IFM? (*What's in it for me?*) question in the second line of my letter: *'we can save you a considerable amount of money'*.

And with the minimum of changes, I've moved all the original 'opening paragraph' details further down in my letter to where the I=Interest details more effectively belong.

Let's take one of those opening paragraphs from the sample dozen that I gave you above. Let's work it through to a second and third paragraph, carefully applying the I = Interest factor and see how it works.

The opening paragraph, selected at random, is the opening paragraph number six: *'Dear reader ... Now I know you are going to find this very hard to believe. But it's true! What's more, for you, it's absolutely free!'*.

And here's how I'm going to progress from this 'attention-grabbing' opening paragraph into developing your interest in the paragraphs that immediate follow it.

Dear reader

Now I know you are going to find this very hard to believe. But it's true! What's more, for you, it's absolutely free!

> You see I was sitting alone in my office last night thinking about you. Actually, I was wondering how on earth could I convince you to use our services next time you have a printing requirement?

Now this is the bit that I know you are going to find hard to believe - **but suddenly my fairy godmother appeared beside me!** She told me that I was to write a letter to you immediately.

She told me exactly what to say to you in my letter. But you know what fairy godmothers are like when they are standing beside you, don't you?

What a beautiful opening piece of whimsical nonsense! And, of course, no sane person would ever be tempted to send out a Fairy Godmother letter like this to an important potential client, would they? The answer is that, many years ago, a client of mine did exactly this. He sent out a letter like this to about 50 clients and potential clients and it worked a dream for him. In fact, even now, all these years later, people still fondly remind him of his Fairy Godmother. You see, my client's Fairy Godmother successfully captured their attention and held their interest for a very long time.

Again, in this example that I am giving you **the interest is in the detail**.

Once I've captured my readers' attention in the opening paragraph of my sales letter, and held their interest in the paragraph(s) that immediately follow, I'm half way through the AIDA formula! My next job is to create a desire in my readers' mind for the products, services, proposition or special sales offer that I am making to them in my letter.

And then I wrap it all up by concentrating on A = Action.

But before we go any further, let's take a little 'chapter break' and do a quick summing up of what we have learned from the AIDA formula so far.

SUMMARY OF CHAPTER 17:
HERE'S WHAT YOU SAY AND HOW YOU SAY IT

☐ Far and away the most popular international structure that is followed by professional copywriters when they are writing sales letters is AIDA.

☐ AIDA stands for A = Attention, I = Interest, D = Desire and A = Action. You should start your sales letter by capturing your readers' attention. The best way to do this is to use one of the magic words in your opening paragraph.

☐ Once you've captured your readers' **Attention** – even if you've only captured it for a fleeting second – you must follow on immediately and hold their **Interest**. This is the part of the letter where you give them some specific details about your offer or your service. The interest is in the detail.

☐ Many companies get off to a bad start with their sales letters by giving the details first, in the hope that the details will capture their readers' attention. As a general rule, it's far safer, and much more effective, not to give the details in your opening paragraph.

18. NOW IS THE TIME FOR RAW, NAKED DESIRE!

> **'We called him Tortoise because he taught us.'**
> Lewis Carroll, *Alice's Adventures in Wonderland* (1865). Ch.9.

I thought I might capture your attention with a chapter titled *'raw, naked desire'*! Interestingly enough, the 'Desire' part of the AIDA formula is not as easy to create as you might expect.

From experience, I can tell you that the easiest and the most 'responsive' way to introduce the D = Desire factor into your sales letter is to press the *'fear of loss'* button.

In my million Euro letter, I do this over two paragraphs when I say:

> Now, I do have one little stipulation, I'm afraid. You see, have you ever stood outside your local post office at 10am in the morning with a million Euro in crisp 20 Euro notes in an expandable brown brief case? No! Well let me tell you, it's not very safe! Anyone can mug you.

> So I'm only going to wait for you for five minutes... not a minute more. At exactly 10.05am, if you don't turn up, I'm going to leave. And I'm going to go to the next post office where I've already invited somebody else to meet me at 10.30am that morning.

Effectively, if you don't turn up, you could lose a million Euro!

Now some products and services are so desirable in themselves that they don't have to press the *'fear of loss'* button at all. Instead, all the writer has to do is heap on the desirable factors, each one reinforcing what went before and all culminating in an irresistibly desirable sale offer. For example, the moment I saw my *Alfa Romeo* Spider motor car in the showroom, I wanted it. The sales rep didn't have to say anything – anything at all – I wanted it immediately. And oddly enough, when I brought a photograph of it along to my very respectable bank manager to negotiate a loan from him to buy the car, he wanted it too! He immediately circulated the photograph around all his colleagues in the bank and, almost without exception, I got the thumbs up sign from them all. It was the fastest loan approval I ever got in my life.

It's easy for people who sell cars, holidays and fashion clothing – even jewellery – to create the appropriate desire factor in a sales letter, but most products or services are not so blatantly desirable as these. Let's say you are selling something very practical like a life assurance policy – which only pays out if you die – or blocks and bolts for the building trade. The easiest way to create the desire factor in these two cases is to apply the *'fear of loss'* principle.

And Okay, I won't quite go far as to recommend that you resort to the tactics that one pushy insurance policy sales man is reputed to have used when he wrote to a potential customer and said:

> Think about it overnight, and let me know your decision when you wake up in the morning. That, of course, is **'IF'** you wake up in the morning.

But what you could say, in the case of the blocks and bolts supplier, is something like:

> If you place your order with me before 12 noon today, I can guarantee you that I will have it delivered to your site before 10am tomorrow.

And, in the case of our pushy friend, the insurance sales person, you could say something along the lines of:

If you contact me about this before next Friday, I can guarantee you that you won't have to do a medical test to secure these very attractive terms.

Some sales letters writers refer to this D = Desire part of their sales letter as 'the call to action' or the CTA. And, in many ways, that's exactly what the *'fear of loss'* motivator is: a call to action.

I can't count how many times I've sat in on creative brainstorming sessions in marketing and advertising agencies, where creative ideas are flying all over the place and nobody is getting anywhere very fast. What often happens in situations like this is that each person vies with the other to come up with something more colourful, more complicated or more expensive than the last idea. And unless the group leader carefully keeps everybody under control, in no time at all the creative ideas will have crossed the sanity-threshold and entered into the world of absolute impractical fantasy.

Then somewhere in the background, at the stage when everybody is having great fun, you hear the group leader's exasperated cry of *'but where's the call to action?'*. That's because he or she knows from long experience that, without a strong call to action, the sales letter, or the direct mail pack, is not going to work as well as it should.

Here's a half-dozen examples of call to action sentences that play up the *'fear of loss'*:

◊   Seats are allocated on a first-come, first-served basis only.

◊   This is our *'Monday Special'* offer and it's definitely only available from 9am to 5pm today!

◊   We've only six apartments with balconies available, so if you want to snap one up, please contact me immediately.

◊   Our next shipment is not due until after Christmas, so if you'd like to present the 'man in your life' with one of these magnificent gift items for Christmas, you must place your order with us immediately.

◊   Last time we made this special wine offer, we were cleared out of stock in 24 hours.

◊ Blue is our most popular colour, so if you're thinking of choosing blue, my advice to you is to telephone me immediately.

FREE GIFTS

Some companies use free gifts to enhance the desire factor.

For example: *'If you order before the end of the month you get a free travel clock'*, or whatever. Free gifts are great quick-response motivators and they work very well for some – but not all – companies and products.

For example, the 'blocks and bolts' supplier would certainly enhance his offer if he promised to include an extra free 500 bricks with all deliveries made this week. The insurance salesman could offer a free calculator *'so that you can work out for yourself all the money you can save on this policy if you move quickly'*. The list of desirable free gift ideas is endless but here's a half a dozen that, over the years, have certainly motivated me:

◊ You get two for the price of one, if you order before a specified date.

◊ A free laptop carry-bag with every laptop purchased this month.

◊ Everybody who responds before a specified date gets an opportunity to win a fabulous holiday in the sun.

◊ Here's a special invitation to a private preview of all the fabulous sales bargains that will be available to the public next week.

◊ Here's a fabulous remote control racing car, complete with batteries and all ready to go. But it can't go anywhere without the remote control. Call us and we'll deliver the missing remote control to you.

◊ Here's the details of a fabulous show that's coming to town. Call us if you'd like us to send you two free tickets for yourself and your partner.

As I mentioned above, the list of free gift ideas is endless. But be careful! Free gifts and incentive offers don't work for every product and certainly don't work with every special offer you make in a sales letter.

For example, if I wrote to you and told you that I had a very special bargain to offer you – a bargain offer so unbelievably good that I am confidently expecting to be sold out of stock within the next 24 hours. And I then went on to offer you a free watch with every item sold. What would you think? Most people in their sub-conscious mind would think: *'if this bargain is so unbelievably good, why does he have to offer me a free watch as well?'*. The inclusion of the free watch somehow diminishes the attractiveness of the offer itself.

There's no hard and fast rule about which sales letter offers become more desirable with the addition of a free gift and which offers are diminished by the inclusion of a free gift. The best way to approach it is to use your common sense. What some companies do is test their sales letter offers with, and without, the desirable free gift on two different segments of their mailing list and monitor the results carefully to see what, if any, difference the free offer makes to the response levels to their sales letter.

Something that you should always be aware of when using a **personal** free gift incentive is the *'bribe'* perception.

Some people, in both the public and private sector, are fearful about accepting services or products that come embellished with offers of very attractive personal free gifts. In fact, the more attractive the personal gift that my clients want me to offer to the respondents to my sales letter, the more my mind focuses in on the possibility that it may be seen by the recipient, or someone else in his/her company, as a bribe. If this happens, they simply won't respond to the sales letter.

A good client of mine, who deals exclusively with the head of departments in legal and accountancy practices, was very conscious of this 'bribe-perception' problem, when he came up with a novel way of using free gifts as a call to action to get these people to respond quickly to his sales letters.

Instead of thinking **big** about what personal free gifts he should offer these powerful people, he thought small ... very small. And he developed a wonderful 'Friday' sales letter campaign that, for sheer ingenuity and for the ability to *'put yourself in the reader's place'*, deserved the huge success that he achieved with it.

His 'Friday' sales letter campaign worked like this:

Every Friday, a letter would arrive on his clients', and potential clients', desks proudly announcing that today is Friday! The ingenuity was imbedded in the announcement. On the first Friday the letter, loudly proclaimed: *'By Gum, It's Friday!'*.

And when the Head of the Department went on to read the rest of the letter, he or she was happily told that *'because it's Friday, we're celebrating! So, if you place an order with us today, we'll send you around, by personal carrier, a packet of Wine Gums!'*.

A packet of Wine Gums!

There's no way that a packet of Wine Gums, which cost only a few cents to buy, could ever be interpreted by these powerful people as being a bribe. In fact, it was so harmlessly outrageous that a sizeable percentage of the recipients thought it was good fun. So much so, that many of them entered into the good spirit of things and placed a Friday order with my client. And yes! They got their packet of Wine Gums personally delivered to them without a moment's delay.

The letter worked so well that it took on a life of its own. And on every first Friday of the month, my client sent out a different offer under various different messages of jubilation:

◊ *'Holy Mint, it's Friday!'* – The offer was a packet of *Polo Mints* (the ones with the hole in them)

◊ *'Great Crunchie, it's Friday!'* – The offer was a delicious chocolate *Crunchie*

◊ *'By Mars, it's Friday!'* – The offer was a mouth-watering *Mars* bar

◊ *'Time Out, it's Friday!'* – The offer was (my favourite) a *Time Out* bar.

Those were sweet days, if you'll pardon the pun. And my client and I had endless fun visiting sweet shops and thinking up zany promotional messages as we sampled the different selections of sweets and confectionery on offer. The rule was: nothing too big – every deliciously desirable gift we offer must cost only a few cents.

It worked for the simple reason that my client was astute enough to understand the response pulling-power of the *'fear of loss'* – or *'call to action'* – factor in a sales letter. And, at the same time, he was wise enough to know that, if his free gift incentive wasn't an obvious fun item, then it could be perceived in a totally negative light as being a bribe by this powerful decision-making group of customers.

There is a lesson to be learned from this little D = Desire story. It is: the value of the personal gift (or call to action) can have an inverse relationship to the wealth of the recipient.

It's an interesting concept, isn't it? And it's a concept that could save you a considerable amount of money, if you are ever faced with the conundrum of trying to select a personal free gift that will appeal to that fabled *'man who has everything'*. Instead of thinking 'big & expensive', turn your mind to thinking 'small & interesting' and you could have the makings of a very successful *'call to action'* in your hands.

Now, having captured your readers' **Attention** at the outset of your sales letter, having held their **Interest** in the following paragraphs, and gone on to create successfully **Desire** in their minds to buy – or to find out more about – your product or service, the next, and the final, step of structuring your very persuasive sales letter is for you to make them take **Action.**

A = ACTION

Action is the final step of the AIDA formula and you should never confuse this A = Action section of your letter with the *'call to action'*, which I have referred to above when I was discussing the D = Desire section of the AIDA formula.

In many ways, A = Action is the simple part of your letter. 'Simple', because, quite simply, what you are doing here is telling your reader what action you now want them to take.

◊   If you want them to buy, you tell them how to buy

◊   If you want them to contact you, you tell them how to contact you

◊   If you want them to meet you, you tell them how to meet you

◊   If you want them to look at your attached catalogue, you tell them to look at your attached catalogue

◊   If you want them to make a donation to charity, you tell them
     to make a donation to charity.

Simple, isn't it? And yet ... and yet ... and yet! This is the part of
the letter that brings out the shyness in so many writers. What I
always tell my workshop participants when I'm telling them
about this stage of the AIDA formula is: *'The road to Heaven is
paved with the bodies of dead reps ... who never made it!'*.

And the reason why they never quite made it through those
pearly gates is because **they never asked for the sale!** It's true of
so many Irish sales people, I'm afraid, and I'm sure that it must be
true of others too.

Again and again, I see it happening with salespeople who
successfully manage to get into my office. At the initial stage and,
indeed, for most of the presentation, the salesperson does a
wonderful job for their company. For starters, he or she
completely ignores my polite initial refusals and insists on
presenting their case to me with superb skill and smiling
affability. They show me how everything works. They eagerly
explain how this little widget is going to make my life so much
easier. They gently pour scorn on the competition's little offering
and carefully compare prices to prove to me beyond all doubt that
what they are trying to sell me is the best – the very best – in
terms of quality, reliability and value in the marketplace.

It's all good heady stuff. Things are looking good. Because,
while I certainly don't want to buy, I have been mesmerised by
their sales pitch and I am momentarily at a loss for words to say
'No', or I simply don't want to disappoint them after such a
friendly sales presentation – during which I'm often given to
understand that I am their lifelong soul-mate.

And then, lo and behold, my salvation comes, straight from the
salesperson's mouth, so to speak, when they say something like:
'There! I'll leave it with you and you can think about it'.

At this stage, my big ears pick up immediately and even
Noddy would be put to shame by the way I rapidly come to life
and nod my head vigorously in agreement with them. I become
filled with the joys of life and good feelings among fellow men as
I enthusiastically say, *'Yes ... yes ... yes, you leave it with me and I'll
think about it'*. Sometimes I go so far as to ask them to leave all

their brochures with me. For good measure, I often ostentatiously put their business card in a very visible place and murmur positive sounding words like *'I'll put it there so that I'll know where to contact you when I need you'*. In short, I do anything – anything at all – to get rid of them politely.

It's all done so politely that everybody is happy. But do you know what? They may not make that sale! Because I haven't promised to do anything other than contact them **when** I need them.

All too often, this is exactly what happens in the A = Action part of sales letters. Time and time again I find sales letters ending with words like *'don't hesitate to contact us if you need more information'* ... or ... *'we'll ring you during the coming weeks to discuss your requirements'*.

The first of the options above is easy for me to deal with because they are, in effect, telling me that I don't need to contact them if I don't need more information. So 'inertia' is the name of the game. The second option is an easy 'inertia' one too, because the moment I read that somebody is going to contact me over the coming weeks I know that I can safely junk the letter in the waste bin. No immediate action has been requested of me in the sales letter and, deep down, I know that 99 times out of 100 nobody will ever call me!

A very successful American salesman once explained to me is that one of the reasons why he is so successful at closing a sale is because he always ends up his sales pitch with these eight simple words: *'How many will I put you down for?'*.

I guess if I were faced with this very specific question, I'd have to immediately sit up and say *'Hey, whoa, hang on, wait a minute, I haven't even decided to buy one!'*. And my American friend assures me that he can take this kind of response in his stride by saying something like: *'Oh! Tell me what you are not sure about, etc, etc, etc?'*. And the selling process (in his case, his successful selling process) continues.

For your sales letter to be successful, you need, like my American friend, to be very specific at the end. You need to say something like: *'Here's how you order'* or you need to be specific like: *'I'll call you next Friday morning before 10am'* (and make it your business to make that call).

You must make it as easy as possible for me to take action or respond to you instantly ... now ... immediately while I still have your letter in my hands. Give me call-free telephone numbers, free post reply envelopes, fax numbers, email addresses, personal mobile phone numbers. Give me them all!

In my million Euro letter I finish up by telling you:

I'll see you outside your local post office at 10am on your birthday. Make sure you keep the time free. In fact, why not mark the appointment in your diary now, while the time, '10am', is still fresh in your mind.

It's quite specific about what I want you to do. Of course, if I knew where you lived I could be far more specific. For example, I could say that I'll see you outside your local post office in Sandymount, or at the bottom of Slaney Hill, Enniscorthy or whatever.

To get the best A = Action in your sales letter, you must believe boldly in your product and not be afraid to be quite specific in telling your readers what exactly you want then to do. Don't fudge! Be specific!

SUMMARY OF CHAPTER 18
HERE'S WHAT YOU SAY AND HOW YOU SAY IT

- ☐ Most of us sell down-to-earth products and services, so we have to work hard to create desire for them in our customers' minds. One way of creating desire is to play up the *'fear of loss'* factor.

- ☐ Incentives can play a useful role in enhancing the desire to respond. However, beware of going too big with a personal incentive. If you go too big, it may be seen as a cover-up for a poor quality/value product. It may also be seen as a personal bribe, and many people will run a mile away from anything that has connotations of personal bribery.

- ☐ 'Fun' incentives can, and do, work well.

- ☐ Many sales letter writers' fail, out of shyness or a lack of belief in the merits of their offer, to press the A = Action button strongly enough at the end of their sales letters. Some don't press it at all, and then wonder why the response they receive is not up to their expectations.

☐   So no matter how tired you are coming up to the end of writing your sales letter, always check – and double check – that you've strongly pressed the A = Action button.

19. PUT YOURSELF IN YOUR READER'S PLACE

> 'I haven't opened it yet', said the White Rabbit, 'but it seems to be a letter, written by the prisoner to – to somebody.'
> 'It must have been that,' said the King, 'unless it was written to nobody, which isn't unusual, you know.'
> Lewis Carroll, *Alice's Adventures in Wonderland* (1865), Ch.12.

Let's put ourselves in our readers' place in this chapter and see whether we can learn anything from them that might help us in our efforts to produce very persuasive sales letters.

One beautiful, warm summer morning on Thursday, 15 June 2000, the first summer of the century, a headline in *The Irish Times* newspaper caught my attention. It read:

One-quarter of Irish adults are functionally illiterate.

As a copywriter who makes his living out of people reading the sales letters that I write, the moment I read this headline, I immediately began to sit up and pay attention to this article. I wanted to know more. I wanted to find out who are these people who are functionally illiterate? More importantly, I wanted to check in and make sure that this 25% of functionally illiterate Irish adults were not among my clients' customers. So I read the article from top to bottom. And the more I read, the more I simply didn't believe what I was reading.

The very first paragraph of the article informed me that:

Some 25 per cent of Irish adults are functionally illiterate and approximately another 20 per cent can perform only simple reading and writing tasks ...

The Irish Times, Thursday, 15 June 2000.

Twenty-five percent are functionally illiterate and another 20% can perform only simple reading tasks! Now I didn't have to be a mathematical genius to add these two percentages together and come up with the simple mind-boggling possibility that 45% of the adult population in Ireland may have difficulty reading my sales letters and a disconcertingly high percentage of these could not read my letters at all!

My first reaction was that this could not be true. I simply couldn't believe that Ireland – the country that prides itself on producing so many literacy geniuses: Swift, Yeats, Joyce, Beckett and so many more – could have such a proportionately high adult literacy problem.

But the article confirmed my worse fears by telling me that these statistical figures were the results of a final report of the international adult literacy survey carried out by the Organisation for Economic Co-operation and Development (OECD). Now, whatever you might think or say about the results of many different surveys that are published nowadays, there is one thing that I can assure you about OECD surveys – they are about the best you can get.

At that stage, there was absolutely no doubt in my mind that the figures that I was reading about were correct. But I still wasn't convinced that I was getting the correct overall picture. Somewhere in the back of my mind, there was a little voice telling me to *'be careful'*.

Maybe these figures only referred to certain segments of the population – the very old, or the very young or the dropouts from school. But even if this were the case, deep down, I felt that 45% was highly questionable.

Because if this is correct, do you know what this means for the Irish market, at the very least? It means that, if I send out 1,000 sales letters to a random selection of Irish adults, before I even start calculating what kind of percentage return I should expect from this mailing, I'm going to have to write off the response-pulling-power of the better part of half my letters. I'll have to do this on the basis that many people in my target group will either not be able to read my letters at all, or else they will find reading them a very difficult chore.

To put it crudely, some 250 letters out of every 1,000 that I send out in the Irish marketplace are a complete waste of time and money. Huh!

If this logic of mine is correct, then every 1% response (10 replies from every 1,000 letters that I send out) that I get to my sales letters in Ireland could be interpreted as being a 1.33% response from those who read them. Because the reality is that only 75% of my target group could even read them.

Then somewhere in the back of my mind, another little bell started tinkling. You see, over the years, I've always noticed something about the sales letters that I write for clients. I've noticed that, on the few occasions that my sales letters have been used *both* in Ireland and America, as a rough rule of thumb, the American response level was always approximately double the response level that the letters achieved in Ireland.

I could never understand why this happened and I simply put it down to the fact that maybe Americans like the Irish *'blarney'* style of copywriting. Although secretly, I was never very happy with this conclusion of mine, because American copywriters have written some of the best sales letters I have ever seen. When it comes to *'blarney'*, some American copywriters could certainly teach Irish copywriters a lesson or two.

So I became curious! Immediately, I wanted to find out how the United States compared with Ireland in this OECD international literacy survey? So I compared the average score achieved on the prose literacy scale by the United States with that achieved by Ireland and discovered that the Americans came out considerably ahead of the Irish. Hmmm! Could it be, I asked myself, that one reason why an identical sales letter of mine was able to achieve a higher percentage response level in America was simply because the Americans were better able to read it?

But, still, there was a niggling little question mark in the back of my mind about who exactly was included in the survey and exactly what kind of literacy skills the survey measured in the different countries.

Without further delay, I contacted the OECD publications office and bought the full text of the survey. And I settled down to a long and interesting read. The very first thing that I noticed was that, in scope, the survey covered the population aged between 16 and 65 in each of the different countries. So the results certainly didn't refer to the very old, or the very young or the dropouts from school. What the survey – and the figures – referred to was, in effect, the working population in each of the countries covered. Okay, the very old and the very young segments of the survey population did pull the final 'averages' one way and another. But the average figures presented in the survey clearly told me that 45% of the working population in Ireland are, to use my own words: *'literacy-challenged'*! To understand more fully what exactly this means, and how it can impact on the success of your sales letters, it's worth your while to have a quick look at how this OECD report defined *'literacy'*.

LITERACY

Literacy is defined in this OECD report as a particular capacity and mode of behaviour:

> The ability to understand and employ printed information in daily activities at home, at work and in the community – to achieve one's goals, and to develop one's knowledge and potential.
>
> *Literacy in the Information Age*, Final report of the international adult literacy survey, OECD.

Literacy, in the survey, is measured under three different categories (domains) of literacy skills:

◊ Prose literacy

◊ Document literacy

◊ Quantitative literacy.

Let's have a closer look at each of these categories.

Prose literacy is the knowledge and skills needed to understand and use information from texts, including editorials, news stories, brochures and instruction manuals.

The easiest level 1 task in this prose literacy testing undertaken by the survey organisers directs the respondents to look at a medical label to determine *'the maximum number of days you should take this medicine'*. The label contains only one reference to number of days and this information is clearly located under the heading 'dosage'. The reader must go to this part of the label and locate the phrase: 'Not longer than 7 days'.

Effectively, what we are talking about is a bottle of aspirin.

Here's what the overall comparative distribution of literacy levels outcome of the test was for prose literacy levels:

Percentage of the population aged between 16 - 65 at each prose level (1994 - 1998)

Ranking Order	OECD Country
1	Sweden
2	Norway
3	Finland
4	The Netherlands
5	Canada
6	Australia
7	New Zealand
8	Denmark
9	USA
10	Belgium (Flanders)
11	Germany
12	Switzerland
13	UK
14	Ireland
15	Czech Republic
16	Switzerland (Italian)
17	Switzerland (German)
18	Hungary
19	Slovenia
20	Portugal
21	Poland
22	Chile

Source: OECD Report - Literacy in the Information Age 2000.

For one, I certainly found a large number of big surprises in this aspect of the survey. I definitely didn't think that the UK and Ireland would end up so low in the Prose literacy league – in 13th and 14th places respectively.

Mind you, when I mentioned this to a client of mine in the International Newspapers Marketing Association (INMA), she informed me that this ranking table, for the European countries at least, didn't surprise her at all. You see, it's long been known among newspapers publishers that the further north you go in Europe, the more newspapers per person are read by the population. And the further south you go, the less newspapers per person are read by the population. So my newspaper friend was not at all surprised to see three northern European Scandinavian countries up there at the top of the list.

The report also measured Document literacy and Quantitative literacy.

2. Document literacy is the knowledge and skills required to locate and use information contained in various formats, including job applications, payroll forms, transportation schedules, maps, tables and charts.

One level 1 document task in this section asks the reader to identify from a chart the percentage of teachers from Greece who are women. The chart displays the percentage of women teachers from various countries. Only one number appears on the chart for each country so, as you can see, the task was very straightforward and, indeed, simple.

Compared with their performance in the Prose table, in the Document literacy ranking things went from bad to worse, insofar as the USA and Ireland were concerned. The USA featured in 9th position in the Prose table and 14th in the Document literacy ranking table. Ireland featured in 14th position in the Prose table and in 17th place in the Document literacy ranking table, while the UK featured in 13th place in the Prose table and 15th place in the Document literacy ranking table.

In the Quantitative literacy table, both Ireland and the UK featured in their lowest respective positions of all.

3. Quantitative literacy is the knowledge and skills required to apply arithmetic operations, either alone or sequentially to numbers embedded in printed material, such as balancing a chequebook, figuring out a tip, completing an order form or determining the amount of interest on a loan from an advertisement.

The easiest quantitative task in this section asks the reader to complete an order form. The last line in the form reads: 'Total with Handling'. The line above it says 'Handling Charge $2.00'. The reader simply has to add the $2.00 handling charge to the total of $50.00 entered on the previous line to indicate the cost of the order. In this task, one of the numbers is stipulated; the operation is easily identified from the word "total"; and the operation does not require the reader to perform the "borrow" or "carry over" function of addition. Moreover, the form itself features a simple column format, further facilitating the task for the reader.

The results of this simple task of adding $50 and $2 were that Ireland ranked in the **18th** position, the UK ranked in the **16th** position, while the USA ranked in **14th** position in the survey.

Of course! Of course! Of course there are all kinds of *caveats*, warnings and, indeed, dangers about using information like this to try and make judgements that are cast in stone about the literacy abilities of people living in different countries. Keep in mind that the 'task examples' that I have outlined are level 1 tasks only, and these are far and away the simplest tasks in each category. It gets more complicated as you move up from level 1.

The sole reason – and it is the only reason – why I am presenting these few brief statistics here is to alert my readers to the simple fact of life that literacy problems can – and do – exist to a greater or lesser extent in different countries. And the number of illiterate people living in different countries may be far greater than you might expect it to be.

More recently, in the summer of 2002, a headline in one of the Irish Sunday newspapers caught my attention. This headline read:

Are you able to read this page?

It was an article on 'health matters' in Ireland by Kate O'Flaherty, *Sunday Tribune*, 16 June 2002, drawing attention to the fact that a lack of basic literacy skills can have a negative effect on a person's health. The Mater Hospital in Dublin reported that one in five people fails to keep outpatient appointments, placing extra cost and time pressures on an already over-stretched system. The article pointed out that there may be many reasons for this, but a lack of literacy skills is a contributory factor. It appears that many patients simply didn't understand the written instructions that were provided to them by doctors and hospital staff.

The article went on to say, 'Some specific examples from various studies appear unbelievable but, to demonstrate how difficult it is for people at high literacy levels to understand the problem, in one survey over 40% of patients did not understand the medical direction *"take on an empty stomach"*.'

It was that **'over 40%'** reference that captured my attention.

Because by my arithmetic, 'over 40%' falls into the same ballpark area as the 45% total figure that is referred to in the earlier Irish Times headline: *'Some 25% of Irish adults are functionally illiterate and approximately another 20% can perform only simple reading and writing tasks'.* (25% + 20% = 45%).

So we have a literacy problem, dimension, factor, call it what you may, on our hands that we must take into consideration when we are trying to write a sales letter that will be read by as many people as possible.

If we accept that people who are functionally illiterate (25% in Ireland) are not going to read our sales letters, what about those who can only perform simple reading and writing tasks? Are we going to write these people off as well? You see, if we can possibly hold on to them, we'll immediately increase our chances of success by as much as 20% in Ireland and 8% in Sweden – the OECD country that ranks at the top of the list with the highest score on the test. But how are we going to hold on to this sizeable percentage of the population?

The answer is by using the *'Ladybird book'* approach.

Do you remember *Ladybird* books? *Ladybird* books are those wonderful children's books that you read when you were first learning how to grapple with the written word. Today, all over the world, parents and teachers still read *Ladybird* books to their children and to their very young pupils every single day of the year.

That's because *Ladybird* books are so easy to read. They use big text. They use simple words. They use pictures and colours to support the words. 'Big' and 'simple' and 'easy to look at'. That's what the words and the text and the pictures in *Ladybird* books are all about.

Hey! Where have you heard this before? You've heard **'Big'** before from me when I told you earlier in this book that *'money is short-sighted'*. Back in **Chapter 13**, when I introduced you to the concept that money is short-sighted, I was referring to the fact that, as people get older, their eyesight fades. And I explained that one sure-proof way of making sure that you don't exclude the 40+ age group from enjoying reading your sales letters is to write *big*!

Well now, the reason why I recommend you to write 'big' is even bigger! Because, not only will big text help those with fading eyesight to read your all-important sales message, but it will also help everybody between the ages of 16 and 65 who have low literacy skill levels to read your sales letters.

And do you remember what I said about *'simple'* and *'easy to look at'*?

Back in **Chapter 10** of this book, I advised you to keep your sentences short and to keep your paragraphs short. I also emphasised that you should also keep a very close eye on the 'appearance' of your letter. My simple message to you was: *'Try and keep everything simple to read and easy to look at'*.

Remember the good advice that our wise friend Aristotle gave us?

Style to be good must be clear. Clearness is achieved by using words that are current and ordinary.

I guess what we are talking about here is the old copywriter's formula: KISS! And what KISS stands for is this: *'Keep it Simple Stupid!'*.

The secret of writing a very persuasive sales letter is to 'kiss' your readers at all times. Keep it simple. Bearing in mind the eyesight difficulties that some of your readers will have, plus the literacy difficulties that other readers will have, it's *you*, I'm afraid, that may end up being the 'stupid' one, if you choose to ignore these two simple realities of the marketplace. Ignore them at your peril!

SUMMARY OF CHAPTER 19:
HERE'S WHAT YOU SAY AND HOW YOU SAY IT

☐ In Ireland, some 25% of the adult population are functionally illiterate and a further 20% of adults between the ages of 16 and 65 can perform only simple reading and writing tasks. In the UK, the percentage figures for both of these categories are somewhat similar.

☐ Further afield in the US, and in other countries, the literacy levels may be much better than in Ireland, but the fact remains that, no matter what country the recipients of your sales letter live in, there will always be people who will have difficulty reading your sales communications.

☐ That's why the old advertising and marketing motto 'KISS' (*Keep it Simple Stupid!*) has a useful role to play in helping us to reach out to the widest possible readership with our sales letters.

☐ Stick to what I call the *Ladybird* book approach and you'll never go far wrong.

☐ Remember also the advice that Aristotle, one of the wisest communicators of all time, gave us when he said: *'Style to be good must be clear. Clearness is achieved by using words that are current and ordinary'.*

20. PICTURE THIS!

'What's the use of a book', thought Alice, 'without pictures or conversations?'
Lewis Carroll, *Alice's Adventures in Wonderland* (1865), Ch.1.

Pictures – word-pictures – can be a very effective way of enhancing your sales message in your sales letters. Never underestimate the power of using 'word-pictures' in a sales letter because they can make a very memorable impact on your readers. And the extraordinary thing about a good word-picture is that sometimes your readers will remember them for the rest of their lives.

Here's a little exercise that I use in my training workshops that will give you an immediate insight into just how difficult the whole process of communicating with the written word is and how powerful the power of word-pictures can be if – and only if – they are described correctly.

What I do is I draw the following picture on a flip-chart that is turned away from my participants so that nobody in the room can see it. And when I finish drawing the picture, I invite one volunteer to come up and admire it. I then ask the volunteer to describe the picture aloud to the rest of the participants and I ask them all to draw the picture that my volunteer is describing on a sheet of paper.

Before we start, there are a couple of ground-rules that I explain carefully to everyone. These are:

◊   The volunteer must describe exactly what they see and, under
     no circumstances, can they use their hands to assist with the
     description. Neither are they allowed move their head or eyes
     to suggest which way any object in the picture is leaning.
     Simply put, my volunteer must impart verbal information to
     the listeners, nothing more

◊   For their part, the listeners are not allowed talk, ask any
     questions or move their bodies. They must do nothing more
     than draw the picture that is being described to them.

So far so good, now here's the picture that I draw:

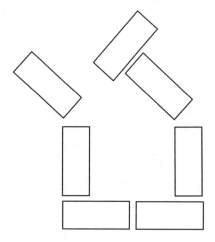

Now, you might like to try out this exercise on some of your
friends or work colleagues and see what happens.

In 99 cases out of a 100, when my volunteers describe the
picture without using any body movement whatsoever, **nobody**
in the room can draw the picture accurately. (Mind you, I've
always been fascinated with the half a dozen or so people that I
have met over the years, who are able to accurately draw the
above picture from a verbal description. They must have unique
minds!)

This is what I call Step 1 in drawing the picture and it usually
ends up being a complete failure on the part of all the
participating would-be artists. The interesting thing is that it's
normally the volunteer who is describing my picture who takes

all the blame for the failure. Inevitably, they will say things like *'I must be a poor communicator'*.

And if I ask the volunteer whether they like to have another go at describing the picture to their audience, they are usually quite happy to describe it yet again. And, yet again, the artists usually end up hopelessly puzzled. So without further ado, I then invite my volunteer to progress to Step 2 of drawing the picture.

The good thing about Step 2 is that the ground rules are relaxed somewhat:

◊ The volunteer describes the picture exactly as before, with no hand or body movements and – this is important – may answer questions from the artists.

◊ Although the artists are not allowed move their hands or arms or any part of their body to try and draw examples of the picture in the air, they are allowed to ask questions. They can ask as many questions as they like and the volunteer is allowed to answer their questions. No body movements are allowed to either support the volunteer's description of the picture or to assist the audience's questions.

This sounds a lot easier doesn't it? The artists can ask as many questions as they like and the volunteer will accurately answer all the questions asked.

But, surprisingly enough, it's not at all simple. As a rough rule of thumb, I would say that only about 25% (often far less) of the artists are able to accurately draw the picture by the end of Step 2. This is quite amazing; try it out for yourself and I'll be very surprised if the results of your experiment don't come up exactly the same as mine.

And now we come to the final step of the experiment: Step 3. The Step 3 ground rules are:

◊ The volunteer is allowed use their hands, arms, head, eyes or whatever to support their verbal description of the picture. They can draw the picture in the air in front of the participants with their finger and can answer all the questions put to her.

◊ The audience are also allowed move their bodies, draw pictures in the air and ask as many questions as they like.

It's at this final stage that things begin to come together and about 75% of the artists successfully draw the picture. Mind you, even at this stage, about 25% still can't get it right. And if you don't believe me? Then try it for yourself and see.

Okay! What am I doing? Why do I ask participants in the middle of a workshop on how to write a very persuasive sales letter to see if they can draw a picture? The answer is simple; I'm trying to give them a very practical insight into just how difficult it is to communicate technical or descriptive information by the written word.

Do you remember Step 1 of this exercise, where the volunteer was not allowed use any part of her body to support her verbal description of the picture? The artists were not allowed ask any questions, they simply had to draw a picture of what was being described to them. Step 1 is the same as **written** communications. When you write, you have no control over how your readers will interpret your written message.

In Step 2, questions and answers were allowed but neither the volunteer nor the artists are allowed use any part of their bodies to physically aid the description of the picture. This Step 2 exercise is the same as communicating by **telephone.** In telephone communications, you can talk and ask all the questions you like but you never actually see the person at the other end of the line. So the person hearing the message forms his or her own mental picture of what you are describing and neither of you has any idea whether this picture is a correct one. In the Step 2 process of the picture exercise that I use among my workshop participants, about 25% of the artists get the correct picture.

Step 3, of course, represents **face-to-face** communications. In Step 3 everybody, volunteer and artists, is allowed to talk, to interact, and to use their hands, arms and bodies to help their description and understanding of what the picture should look like. This is the stage where the picture comes together for most people, but a surprisingly high percentage of the participants still can't get it right even at this stage.

But the hardest stage of all is Step 1 – the **written** communication stage. And the lesson to be learned here is that, in written communications, you simply have no idea what kind of picture your reader is drawing in his or her mind about the product or service that your written words are describing to them in your sales letter. They could be forming the wrong picture entirely about you and your company and your promotional offer. And the more complex or technical your offer is, the greater the chances are of the overall picture being distorted in your reader's minds.

Actually, there is a very simple way to describe this picture and over the years I've found that when I describe it this way I get a very respectable level of success from participants. Here's my description:

> The picture is made up of the following capital letters: there are two Ls, an I and a T. Place the two L's facing each other so that they from a big U. Put the I on the top of the left upright of your big U and the T on top of the right upright. Now, imagine that the T is falling in to the centre of your big U. It has smashed against the I on the other side of your big U and the I is just about to topple off to the left. Both the I and the T are toppling over to the left at a 45 degree angle. The impact of the fall is so great that the horizontal line forming the top of the T has been pushed off-centre, so that twice as much of it is on the uppermost right hand side of the falling T than on the lower left which is nearest the I.

> That's the outline structure of the picture. Now let me tell you that each of these capital letters is made up of equal size builder's bricks and there is an equal gap between each brick for the mortar to be filled in. That's the reason why the horizontal brick forming the top of the T got shoved backwards when it hit the I. You see, there's no mortar to hold it together.

Do you see what I'm up to in the above explanation? Most people when they are describing my picture start off by talking about rectangles, with the result that their listeners quickly get confused trying to imagine how all these rectangles come together. Over the years, I've found that, if you start the process by simply talking about four capital letters and later fill in the picture, as it were, by explaining that these capital letters are made of bricks, most people find it easier to follow. And they can readily understand why the top of the 'T' has been pushed off-centre.

THE POWER OF PICTURES

The purpose of this little exercise is to help you to understand how difficult written communication is and what a powerful friend 'word-pictures' can be when you are trying to explain something technical or obscure to your readers. Let me share with you a personal experience of the 'power of pictures' in operation.

Many years ago when I was richer, younger and far more handsome than I am now, I worked as the Head of Human Resources in a large multi-national bank. Mine was a fairly senior position in the bank that called for working late hours. And often, long after everyone else had departed to taste the joys of the local pub, you would find me still sitting in my office wading through the never-ending mountain of paperwork that, somehow or other, always seemed to land on my desk.

One late June evening, the setting sun was pouring through my window, as I was working on some interview notes that I had taken earlier in the day and the telephone on my desk rang. It was the hall porter, who informed me that the chairman of the bank was on the other end of the line asking for me. The chairman was asking for me? Indeed he was.

In a fraction of a second, my mind soared to dizzy heights. Now, at last, I told myself, I was surely going to get proper recognition for my undoubted genius. There was no question about it in my mind; I was going to be promoted beyond my wildest dreams. And the chairman himself was about to tell me the good news. So I grabbed the telephone only to find that *'twas not I'* that the chairman had on his mind, but far more important things (if that could possibly be) concerning the future of the company.

'Robert', the chairman's voice pronounced. *'I want you to do something for me, immediately please'*. And in three or four crisp sentences, the chairman told me exactly what I must do.

It transpired that, on the following morning, there was a shareholders' meeting due to take place. For complicated reasons that I won't get into here, the chairman needed some important documents for this meeting. He didn't expect that he would have to call on these documents, so he hadn't requested them earlier. But something had happened in the media within the last few hours and it had now become a matter of priority for him to have these documents to hand to use, if required, at the following morning's meeting.

My instructions were that I was to go to the confidential document safe in the bank. I was to open the safe. And on top of a pile of papers, I would find a fairly large brown envelope containing all the documents that the chairman required. Once I had these papers in my hands, I was to ring the bank's regular courier company and I was to organise for a courier to collect this envelope from me at my home the following morning and deliver it at 8am to the chairman at the front door of the hotel where the shareholders' meeting was due to take place. I lived quite close to the hotel, so everything was relatively straightforward.

Before he hung up, the chairman emphasised to me that he didn't want any fuss or media attention drawn to him when the courier arrived. All he wanted was a courier to arrive on time on a motorbike and simply hand over the brown envelope to him.

Naturally, I was disappointed to find that my hour for promotion had not yet come. But I consoled myself in the knowledge that I was being entrusted with a vital task upon which the entire future and well-being of the bank could well rest. So, quick as a light, I opened the document safe, grabbed the brown envelope and rang the courier company with my all-important instructions.

I explained to the courier company what exactly was required from them the following morning. I told them that the chairman himself would be waiting outside the front door of the hotel at 8am. The chairman was a well-known public figure, so the person taking my call in the courier company knew exactly whom I was talking about. He assured me that there would be no fuss or bother with the delivery and that the chairman would have the envelope discreetly and efficiently delivered personally into his hands. *'Discretion is the key!'*, he assured me.

The delivery end of things was very straightforward in the courier company man's mind. It was the actual collection from me in my house that he was more concerned about. He wanted to know where exactly I lived and how the courier was to find me the following morning.

Now I live in Lea Road – number 13 Lea Road, Sandymount, Dublin. So I carefully explained to the courier company that it was number 13. To make absolutely sure that he had the correct number I emphasised 'unlucky 13'. And I explained – explained very carefully – to him that my house would be very easy to locate, because outside it would be parked my pride and joy in life: a bright red *Triumph* Spitfire motor car.

I lovingly described my Spitfire in some detail to him. I told him that it was a sports car with a soft-top roof and it had all the bells and whistles that come with sport cars that are the pride and joy of your life. And the courier man carefully wrote it all down and assured me that nobody could possibly miss such a fantastic car like that. Between us, we had a great conversation about the thrills and spills of sport car life.

The following morning, my wife and I were up and about early. And at approximately 7.15am, we heard an almighty rumble outside our window. On looking out, we saw to our amazement a huge 40-foot container truck carefully driving down the very narrow Lea Road. Emblazoned on the side of this massive truck was the courier company's name and logo. Nobody could possibly miss seeing this truck. Nobody could mistake the logo on the side of it. And it stopped right outside our house.

Moments later, there was a knock on the door. Outside were three uniformed courier company employees and the one standing in the middle, who was obviously the boss, wore a smart-looking cap on his head and carried an official-looking clipboard in his hands. He tipped the peak of his cap with his finger and announced: *'We've come to collect the* Triumph *Spitfire, sir'*.

'We've come to collect the Triumph *Spitfire!'*. Yikes!

And the lasting memory, which will remain with me for the rest of my life, was the sight of three rather bemused-looking courier company employees sitting three-abreast in the front cab of that huge container truck, with the man in the peaked cap in the middle holding the chairman's brown envelope in his two hands as the truck rumbled off to the hotel to make its vital delivery.

I learned later that the chairman was not – at all – amused with my delivery arrangements. It seems that the truck rumbled into the forecourt of the hotel. And the envelope was handed down from the window of the driving cab into the chairman's outstretched hands in front of the very eyes of the business media reporters who were there to report on the developments of the shareholder's meeting. Hmmm! So much for my nice discreet delivery arrangements.

How on earth did it all go so terribly wrong? How could the courier company possibly have got it so mixed up? The answer is very simple: **the power of word-pictures!**

You see, I was obviously so proud of my red sport car and I described it with so much enthusiasm that the simple plain brown envelope, which the courier company was meant to collect, paled into complete oblivion. My guess is that the man who took my instructions on the telephone the evening before must have emphasised the red Spitfire in his instructions. He must have had a glorious word-picture in his mind as to how exactly it looked ... shining and gleaming in the early morning sun.

And the following morning, when the next shift looked through their collection worksheets for the morning, the big bright exuberant words *'red* Triumph *Spitfire'*, and whatever other glowing things he said about it, must have jumped off the page and fired their imagination. So off they went with great enthusiasm to collect my Spitfire from my home and deliver it to the chairman at the front door of the hotel.

The reason why I am telling you this story in such detail is because **'word-pictures sell'**. And in this case, they certainly sold my red Spitfire in the imagination of the courier company man who wrote down my instructions. I obviously described it to him with so much enthusiasm in my voice that he jotted down more notes about the red Spitfire than he did about the rather mundane brown envelope. And the moral of this story is that when you are writing a sales letter *'never underestimate the power of word-pictures'*.

AN INVALUABLE TOOL FOR WRITERS OF CHARITY APPEAL LETTERS

For example, during the 'battle of words' period of the American and Iraq standoff in February 2003, the Southern African countries were faced with a looming famine crisis of the most horrifying proportions. But the eyes of the world were on Iraq. Despite the urgency of the international relief agencies appeals, the voices of the starving people in Africa were just not being heard. Worse still! The relief agencies were reporting that their funds were drying up. It seems that nobody was interested in giving to charity in the possible countdown to fighting. Nobody was listening. Everybody was tuned in to the faraway rumblings of war.

One Irish relief agency harnessed the mood of the time with an appeal letter headed:

'The rumblings of war roll louder than the rumblings of hunger.'

In itself, this sentence means nothing. But it certainly created a word-picture and an important platform for the relief agency to explain to its readers in their charity appeal letter that, because the looming war situation was dominating the media, the plight of the starving people in the Southern African countries was not getting the humanitarian attention it deserved.

So if you ever have a difficult story to tell, a complicated product to sell, or you need to capture your reader's attention with a yell, try painting a word-picture in your reader's mind in your sales letter. You'll be surprised at how effective, memorable and distinctive aptly-described word-pictures can be. But a word of caution, always test out the effectiveness of your word-picture on a friend or a colleague before you send it out. Make double-sure that you are not sending out a word-picture that only you can interpret.

SUMMARY OF CHAPTER 20:
HERE'S WHAT YOU SAY AND HOW YOU SAY IT

☐ Face-to-face communication is one of the easiest and most foolproof ways of getting across your message. That's because you have body language to support your communications and you can ask questions and check and make sure that the correct message has been imparted to the receiver. Communicating with the written word is the most difficult method of all, because all you have to support your communication message is words, and you have no immediate way of checking to ensure that the receiver has interpreted your words correctly.

- ☐ If you have a technical or complex product or service to describe to your readers in a sales letter, 'word-pictures' can often make things much easier for everyone.

- ☐ Word-pictures are a double-edged copywriters' tool. They can cut both ways! By this I mean that, if you don't use the correct words in your picture, you may end up painting an entirely different picture in your reader's mind than you intend to. So always check out the effectiveness of your word-picture among your colleagues and friends before you use it in your sales letter.

- ☐ Of course, you could print an actual picture of your product on your sales letter, but a sales letter that contains a printed picture looks more like printed material than a very personal 'me-to-you' letter. In any case, if you are a service provider (for example, a copywriter like me), it's difficult to find a picture that will instantly explain the benefits of your service.

21. STRATEGIES FOR SUCCESS

> 'That's not a regular rule; you invented it just now.'
> 'It's the oldest rule in the book,' said the King.
> 'Then it ought to be Number One,' said Alice.
> Lewis Carroll, *Alice's Adventures in Wonderland* (1865), Ch.12.

Let's talk about strategy. Strictly speaking 'strategy' is such an important key to the success of your sales letters that, as Alice so aptly puts it ... *'it ought to be Number One'.*

Because strategy is something that you should decide on before you ever put pen to paper. Strategy is all about determining how exactly you are going to present yourself or your sales message to your readers. What is your unique selling point (USP)? What is your target audience like? How do you want your target audience to perceive you?

The problem with making strategic decisions like this is that there are so many – sometimes too many – decisions to be made. It's hard to know where to start. And it's hard to know where to stop. I have a very simple method of starting the strategy process moving. It's so simple that I mentally call it 'Strategy Rule Number One'.

And the way my Strategy Rule Number One works is as follows: Always ask yourself, right from the outset, *'What do I want this sales letter to achieve for me?'*.

For example:

◊   Do I want it to get me a job?

◊   Do I want it to make new/existing customers contact me immediately?

◊   Do I simply want it to educate people about my new service or product?

◊   Do I want it to sell a very specific product for me?

◊   Do I want it to open a door for a follow-up call by a rep?

◊   Do I want it to raise money for charity?

◊   ... Or whatever!

Sounds easy, doesn't it? Actually, it's far more difficult than you might think. Because what I generally find is that what most people, and just about all companies, want their sales letters to achieve is a vast multitude of things for them. Usually they want it to achieve 'the impossible', with the result that it becomes impossible for me to meet all their requirements within the confines of a one or two-page sales letter.

For example, it's not unusual for a client to tell me that *'I want it to sell ... I want it to educate ... I want it to do a PR job for my company ... I want it to open doors for my reps ... I want it to make money ... I want it to encourage more customers to do business with me ... I want ... I want.... I want!'*.

Start-up companies are usually the most demanding in this area. That's because they are inevitably working to a very tight budget and they have a pressing need to generate cash flow quickly. From a strategic viewpoint, the problem, however, is that if you have a very long list of 'wants' to include in your sales letter, quite simply, you are putting too many demands on your readers. And if your reader finds that you are demanding too much of them, they may go into complete negative mode and reject your sales letter entirely.

So you may need to refine your 'want' list. One very productive way of approaching this problem is to write down all your 'wants' on paper. Once you've got everything down on paper, rank them in order of your immediate priority. Yes! I know this can be difficult but it's amazing what you can achieve when you put your mind to it. Number them in order of priority ... one, two, three, etc.

Next comes the limitation exercise, I'm afraid. Because the more you can limit your 'wants' in your letter, the clearer your call to action will be in your reader's mind. If you can limit it to three, you're doing well, because most people can easily absorb three concepts or three new ideas at the one time. If you can limit it to **one**, you are doing superbly and you have the makings of a very strong 'Unique Selling Point' (USP) or 'Call to Action' (CTA) in your sales armoury.

However, it's not easy to limit it to one. In fact, sometimes it can be darn hard to limit it to one. But in all my years' experience of working with, and writing, sales letters, I have learned the invaluable lesson that, if you can limit it to one – one crystal clear call to action – you considerably increase your chances of success.

JUST ONE WANT!

Let me give you a crystal clear example of what I mean.

Olwen Kelleghan is a very bright, intelligent honours college graduate. Now, the time has come for Olwen to get her first job in her chosen career. Sure, she has worked on summer jobs, student jobs, work assignments and projects before. But now that she has graduated, she wants to put her foot firmly on the first rung on the ladder to her successful career. In a nutshell, Olwen needs an employer in 'her chosen field' to employ her.

I guess her 'want' list could have been something like this:

◊   Get a job

◊   Get one quickly

◊   A job with prospects

◊   A job with a reputable company

◊   A challenging job

◊   A job that will allow me to use my skills

◊   ... and so on and so forth.

Number one item on the list is: *'Get a job!'*. This is not as easy as you might think, because Olwen's chosen career field is in film production. There are not that many film production companies in Ireland – not many at all! Consequently, there are very few job openings for graduates with Olwen's experience. So few are there, in fact, that she'll be very lucky indeed if she even gets called for one interview. And she certainly won't get a job, if she doesn't get interviews.

Before Olwen has a snowball's chance in hell of landing that all-important first job in her chosen career, she **must** get an interview. With a little bit of intelligent thinking, and with careful consideration, Olwen changed the number one entry on her 'want' list to: *'Get an interview!'*.

Once this strategic change was made, things began to fall into place very quickly. Olwen's list of wants now began to look something like this:

◊   Get an Interview

◊   Even a five-minute interview

◊   Quickly

◊   With a company that can offer me the right kind of job

◊   With prospects.

Olwen quickly drew up a list of companies that she would like to get an interview with and she sent them the following 'gem' of a letter. It's an absolute sparkler! Within 24 hours of mailing it, she got her first call for interview. And yes! She landed herself a job too!

Here's Olwen's letter:

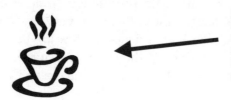

Carefully mounted at the top of Olwen's letter was a beautiful miniature doll's cup and saucer – a real cup and saucer! And tucked loosely into the fold of this letter was a small sachet of instant coffee.

Dear Personalised Name

If you're not convinced by the time you drink this tiny cup of coffee
I'll fly away ... honest!

The enclosed cup of coffee is for you! It's small – **very small** – and the chances are that you'll finish drinking it in far less than five minutes! But that's all the time I need from you.

> Because if I don't convince you in five minutes that I could be a valuable addition to your company, I'll fly away ... **honest!**

My name is Olwen Kelleghan. I'm a 22-year old honours graduate of the Dun Laoghaire Institute of Art, Design & Technology. And I'm looking for a job. Actually, at this stage, all I'm really looking for is an **interview**.

I have a considerable amount of qualifications and skills to offer your company. But I'm very conscious that, on its own, a CV is little more than a list of successes and experiences written down on paper.

It lacks that vital 3-D element that'll help you to see how I can make a very positive contribution towards the future development and success of your company.

> That's why I'd welcome an opportunity to meet you. I'd like to introduce myself to you personally, show you my CV if you wish and some of my work and tell you just a little bit more about the film, video and design production skills that I can offer you.

My home telephone number is 01-XXX XXX. My mobile number is 087 XXX XXX and I can be contacted on either of these numbers at any time. Better still, you might prefer to use the enclosed **'Fax Flyer'** to let me know when you next have five minutes to spare to meet me during your coffee break!

I'm looking forward to hearing from you soon.

Yours sincerely

Olwen Kelleghan

PS In the meantime, I'll keep practising my flying!

Fax Flyer

To: Olwen Kelleghan
               Address
               Address
               Address
Phone: 01 XXX XXX
Mobile: 087 XXX XXX

☐ **Okay Olwen,** I'm not promising you anything, but let's meet!

   Call me on: _____

Tick here for optional extra: Bring the chocolate biscuits!   ☐

☐ **Keep in touch, Olwen,** send me the:
   - Coffee pot   ☐
   - Sugar bowl   ☐
   - Milk jug (tick your preference)   ☐

   ... in a month's time to remind me to contact you to arrange an interview with you.

☐ **Sorry Olwen,** we've no suitable vacancies for a person with your qualifications (and flying skills!).

Name:

Company:

Position:

Date: _____

Fax This Fax Flyer To Olwen Kelleghan on 01-XXX XXXX

Have you noticed something about this wonderful letter? It doesn't contain a CV! Most job applicants enclose a CV when they are looking for an interview. But Olwen deliberately adopted a different strategy. And it worked!

Within 24 hours, she got her first fax flyer reply saying *'Okay Olwen, I'm not promising you anything but let's meet'*. And, as the days went by, she got more. Not surprisingly, many of the fax notices featured little pen-messages saying, in effect: *'Loved your letter ... what a wonderful idea ... etc'*.

Now look carefully at the top left-hand corner of Olwen's letter and you'll see a cup and saucer featured on it. This is where Olwen put both her artistic capabilities and her determination to work. In her original, the cup and saucer were real! Yes! What featured at the top of Olwen's letter was a real miniature china cup and saucer. They were beautiful little miniatures and the cup had been carefully stuck to the saucer and then the combined cup and saucer affixed to the letter. The combined cup and saucer protrude about a centimetre from the letter.

The final touch was a small sachet of instant coffee that was tucked loosely into the fold of the letter, so that it fell out when the letter was opened. This was the coffee to make the tiny cup of coffee that could be drunk in far less than five minutes ... which was all the interview time that Olwen was looking for.

By simply asking the question: *'What do I want this letter to achieve for me?'*, Olwen had identified the strategic platform upon which to create her very persuasive sales letter. Because the more she thought about the question, the more she realised that what she really wanted her letter to achieve for her was an interview ... not a job.

MORE STRATEGIC THINKING IN ACTION

Peter Mercier, who is a client, a very successful businessman, and a good friend of mine, sells, among other things, a wide range of construction membrane products. Some of these membranes go underneath the foundations of buildings; others go under the roof slates. He has many different membranes in his product range; some are reinforced for extra strength, some are lightweight, some have special anti-glare features for working on rooftops in the full glare of the sun, and so on and so forth.

He needed a sales letter (possibly two or three different sales letters) to accompany folders, which contained different sample selections of his range of products, which he planned to deliver to architects, engineers and construction industry 'specifiers' to introduce them to his entire membrane product range.

There were a number of different folders. For example, there was a folder containing the roofing membrane selection. There was a folder containing the building foundation membrane selection and so on. An individual folder could contain anything up to a dozen carefully hand-mounted membrane samples, each approximately the size of, and little more than the width of, a postcard.

As you can imagine, sample folders like this are expensive to produce. Ideally, Peter wanted to get the samples into the hands of architects, engineers and construction industry 'specifiers' who had a need for – or who would use – these products.

Easier said than done! For starters, he had to identify who were those architects, engineers and construction industry 'specifiers' who had a need for – or who would use – these products. Of course, he could have sent the samples to everybody in the different groups. But if he did this, there was a danger that he might waste a considerable amount of money delivering expensive sample selections to people who didn't want them. So the crucial question was *'How do I identify the people who will make best use of my samples?'*.

Peter's 'want list' for what he wanted his sales letter(s) to achieve would probably have shaped up something like this:

◊   Increase sales

◊   By introducing the full product selection to the right people

◊   Emphasise the superior quality of the products

◊   And make my company's name known to the readers

◊   Tell them that they can order these products directly from us

◊   And convey to the reader that we are a reputable stockist of these products

◊   ... And so on.

Number one item on Peter's list is ... increase sales. This is straightforward enough. The prime purpose of Peter's letter is to sell more membranes. The problem is that, before he can sell more membranes, Peter needs to talk to the 'right' people. The key question is how is he going to identify the right people in a cost-effective way?

Peter knew that, if he could only identify the 'right' people and explain to them why the membrane products he sold were of a superior quality, his sales should automatically increase. Identifying the 'right' people was the obvious turnkey to success. Once this strategic decision was made, things began to fall into place very quickly. Peter's list of wants now began to look something like this:

◊   Identify the right people

◊   Give these people the sample folders

◊   Explain the 'superior quality' of the product range to them

◊   And tell them how easy it is to order these products from my company.

After much consideration, he opted for a two-stage marketing strategy. Stage 1 was to identify the right people. And Peter used a very imaginative and cost effective approach to help him achieve his Stage 1 objective. He sent postcards out to all architects, engineers and construction industry 'specifiers'... postcards with a huge difference!

You see one of the interesting things about Peter's samples was that, as I mentioned earlier, they were all postcard size. With a little bit of imagination, two white adhesive labels (one label on one side for the address and the other one on the other side for the short sales message) plus a postage stamp, Peter created some fabulous postcards made out of the membrane samples themselves.

For example: One membrane sample was metallic blue in colour. This was a tough high-quality reinforced polyethylene membrane and sandwiched in the centre of it, for added protection, was a strip of silver foil. Here's what the message on the card said:

ELIMINATE THOSE MOODY BLUES ...
EVERY CLOUD HAS A SILVER LINING ...

INSIDE THIS BLUE SAMPLE OF XYZ ROOFING MEMBRANE,
YOU WILL FIND THAT ALL IMPORTANT SILVER LINING

IF YOU'D LIKE TO SEE THE FULL XYZ RANGE ,
CALL **NECOFLEX IRELAND** ON 01-2876111, FAX 01-2876614

This postcard was sent to everybody on Peter's list. And a week later, they received a second card, made up of a sample of a silver foil membrane that provided sub-floor protection for radon soil gas. Here's what the silver card said:

LOOK FOR THAT SILVER LINING ...
WHENEVER YOU WANT TO BANISH RADON OR METHANE

INSIDE THIS SAMPLE OF XYZ MEMBRANE,
YOU WILL FIND THAT ALL IMPORTANT SILVER LINING

IF YOU'D LIKE TO SEE THE FULL XYZ RANGE,
CALL **NECOFLEX IRELAND** ON 01-2876111, FAX 01-2876614

A week later, they received a third card, which is my favourite, made of a very strong black membrane. And the message on this card read:

THERE'S A RESILIENT BLACK SHEEP IN EVERY FAMILY ...

IF YOU'D LIKE TO SEE THE REST OF THE XYZ HIGH PERFORMANCE MEMBRANES
AND GEOMEMBRANES FAMILY, WE'LL SEND YOU A FREE SAMPLE BOX.

CALL **NECOFLEX IRELAND** ON 01-2876111, FAX 01-2876614

In no time at all, recipients of these post cards began to contact Peter asking for the free sample box. Everybody who contacted him was immediately placed into 'right people' category.

The next steps were to:

◊   Give these people the sample folders

◊   Explain the 'superior quality' of the product range to them

◊   And tell them how easy it is to order these products from Peter's company: Necoflex.

So all the 'right' people (the architects and engineers who contacted Peter after receiving the postcards) received a hand-delivered box of samples. And the very first thing they read when they opened their box was the following marvellous sales letter which introduced them to the 'XYZ Family', highlighting the quality dimension of each member of the family and telling them how easy it is to order any of these quality products.

Mr Robert Hayes-McCoy
Title
Address

Dear Robert

Welcome to the XYZ Family!

As with any other extended family introduction, we can't possibly expect you to remember all the different names and their occupations the first time you meet them, but they all have one thing in common ...

... they're all engineering graduates!

You see, every single XYZ product has been researched and tested to the highest international standards and they have passed these examinations with distinction.

They all speak a common international language too! ... **the language of quality.**

We're a strongly bonded family, and you'll find the family grid on many of the enclosed samples. You'll also find the family silver in your sample box, carefully sealed between two layers of polyethylene for extra protection.

I'd like you to know that everything you see in your sample box can be supplied to you by Necoflex in Ireland.

Call us anytime and we'll be pleased to give you an immediate quotation on any item that you are interested in. And if you place an order with us, we can deliver your exact specifications on-site to anywhere in Ireland.

Yours sincerely

Peter Mercier
Managing Director

PS To keep the introductions within the family, I've asked my daughter, Emma, to personally deliver this sample box into your office.

It's a lovely marketing campaign. And the strategy of using postcards in Stage 1, followed up with this very unusual *'Welcome to the XYZ Family'* sales letter in Stage 2, resulted in Peter's company very quickly becoming one of the largest distributors of XYZ membrane products in Europe.

Sometimes the strategy decision can be very straightforward and simple. It doesn't have to be two-dimensional like Olwen's strategy or in two stages like Peter's strategy.

MAKE ME FEEL SPECIAL!

Here's an example of a bank that used a very simple strategy to take advantage of a 'once off' occasion perfectly. This was a bank that had a very high number of loan customers. They needed a sales letter that they could send to all loan customers coming up to the time when their loan was about to be paid off in full. They wanted to encourage their customers to take out a new loan immediately and simply continue making the same monthly payments as before.

The problem was, and the bank was very aware of this, that some of these loans had been taken out three, four ... even five years previously. And because these customers had excellent monthly repayment records, they had received few communications from the bank over the years of their loan repayments. In a nutshell, they had very little reason to be loyal to the bank.

To complicate matters even further, many of these excellent loan customers probably didn't pay much attention to which bank they had borrowed the money from. Now I know that this last may sound very hard to believe but, actually, there's a very simple reason for this. Some of these loans were used to purchase new cars and it was the car sales rep in the garage who organised the loan and completed most of the paperwork for the customer. The customer simply signed a direct debit form and drove off in their new car. And while the direct debit deduction amount, and the bank's name did, of course, feature on the customer's monthly bank statements, invariably it was the amount of money rather than the source of the fund that received most attention.

In terms of what exactly they wanted this sales letter to achieve for them, the bank's 'want' list went something like this.

◊   Get the customers to take out a new loan

◊   By simply topping up his/her original loan

◊   To an amount equal to, or greater than, the original loan amount.

◊   Advise the customer that all our loans are subject to 'loan approval criteria' (in other words, in line with standard banking practice, the customer has to reapply for the new loan).

Uh Oh! It's that last one – *'advise the customer that all our loans are subject to loan approval criteria'* – that might be just that little bit tricky. After all, the customer has an excellent loan repayment track record with the bank, so he or she might feel that they shouldn't have to re-apply for a new loan. There was a danger that they might feel so peeved about this that they wouldn't be very favourably disposed towards taking out another loan. *'Surely'*, they might say to themselves, *'I deserve better treatment than this?'*.

But this is something that the bank's loan approval department insisted on – all loans must be 'subject to loan approval'. Of course, good customers like these, who have excellent repayment track records with the bank, shouldn't have any great difficulty obtaining loan approval, nevertheless they had to **re-apply** for their loans, and go through the approval system like everybody else.

The more the bank thought about it, the more they realised that they needed to make an important amendment to their original 'want' list. What they needed to do was assure the customer that, despite the lack of correspondence over the years, he/she was definitely very highly regarded in the bank

So a new 'want' was introduced into the number one position on the bank's want list. The revised number one priority of the sales letter was *'we want the customer to feel special!'*. Once this decision was reached, a very interesting adjustment was made to the original want list. The new want list went something like this:

◊   Tell the customer that they are special

◊ Because of their excellent loan repayment record

◊ Invite them to take out a new loan

◊ Advise them that all loans are subject to normal credit criteria – but, because of their excellent repayment record, they are in our *'Privileged Loan Customer'* category.

Note how, despite its exalted sounding name, *'Privileged Loan Customer'* category doesn't actually promise or guarantee anything, so the loan approval department of the bank was happy enough to let the following letter go out.

Name
Address

Date

Dear Mr Hayes-McCoy

Do you remember what you were doing on 21 July 2000?

Because that was the day our bank agreed your loan for €10,000.

And all the time you were enjoying the benefits of your loan, something very important was happening here...

... your credit rating was steadily growing.

And when you make your final loan repayment on 21 July – which is only a short four weeks from now – you will immediately enter our **'Privileged Loan Customer'** category.

That's why I'm writing to you.

I'd like you to know that, subject to our special 'Privileged Customer Credit Approval Criteria', we'll be delighted to give you an immediate loan of up to €10,000 – or even more, if you require it.

What's more, we'll be pleased to give it to a valued customer like you at **SPECIAL TERMS**. It's our way of saying 'thank you' for being a 'Privileged Loan Customer' of our bank and letting you know how much we value your custom.

Have a look at the enclosed brochure ... etc etc.

Not only did this letter make the customer feel remembered, wanted and special but look how well the bank handled the delicate 'subject to loan approval criteria'. They called it *'Privileged Customer Credit Approval Criteria'*. Nice strategic thinking that!

Needless to say, this letter was very successful because the bank took the time, in advance of putting pen to paper, to get the strategy of their sales letter spot-on!

Getting the strategy right is a very important part of creating the success platform for your successful sales letter. To help you to determine your own strategy, in my next chapter I'd like to introduce you to my *'seven rules for reaping results'*.

SUMMARY OF CHAPTER 21
HERE'S WHAT YOU SAY AND HOW YOU SAY IT

☐ The best sales letters – and sometimes the easiest sales letters to write – are those where the writer has clearly identified in advance 'What exactly do I want this letter to achieve **for me?**'.

☐ Never forget, however, that like a successful negotiator who knows that if he asks for too much he'll end up with nothing, a good sales letter should not place too many demands on the reader.

☐ Before you put pen to paper, therefore, you should draw up a 'want list' of what exactly you want your sales letter to achieve for you. Write down everything in a want list!

☐ Organise your want list in order of priority and put numbers beside your different wants: Want 1, Want 2 etc. Next, try limiting your number of wants to a maximum of three and check to see whether your top three wants will achieve most of what you require your letter to achieve. If they don't, then maybe you've selected the wrong top three wants. See if you can rearrange your list of wants.

☐ Sometimes, you might find that the key or the 'trigger' want is not always at the top of your list. For example, the key to Olwen securing a job was first to get a job interview. The key to Peter increasing his sales was to put his samples in the right hands; the key to the bank overcoming the difficulty of insisting that even 'excellent' customers go through their loan approval system was to assure them that they were special. Once you establish the correct key or 'trigger' to put at the top of your want list, your winning strategy quickly falls into place for you.

22. SEVEN RULES FOR REAPING RESULTS

> 'Why, sometimes, I believe as many as six impossible things before breakfast.'
> Lewis Carroll, *Through the Looking Glass* (1872), Ch.5.

RULE 1: KNOW YOUR KEY SELLING POINTS

It's always worth your while to invest time in advance of writing your letter to carefully think about your selling points. Decide, at the outset, what selling points you want to include in your sales letter. Remember, the clearer your selling points, the more effective your letter will be. Likewise, the clearer your selling points, the easier it will be for you to write a successful sales letter.

One of the things that new and potential clients always find unnerving about me is my ability to listen carefully to them while they describe their product or service to me in detail. I take in every word they say. I make careful notes. And I jot down each important thing they mention to me as they talk at length. And I nod. I nod my head wisely as I encourage them to reveal all. Then, when it's all over, I look at them straight in the eyes and ask them very politely: *'Yes! But what exactly does product X do?'*. Alternatively I ask: *'But why on earth would anyone want to buy product X?'*.

And then, for a few dangerous seconds, the client or would-be client looks at me in either one, or a mixture, of the following emotions.

◊   In desperation: 'Surely I've explained this to him.'

◊   In despair: 'Is he not listening to me at all?'

◊   In anger: 'Why am I wasting my time with this guy?'

◊   In exasperation: 'What a stupid question.'

◊   In total disbelief: 'What kind of a fool am I talking to?'

◊   In abject defeat: 'Was my explanation really that bad?'

But I've learnt that, if I'm prepared to stand my ground and suffer all these mixed emotions in silence, I'll usually get a very interesting answer to this question of mine. Because what the client will often do is come straight to the point and give me in one sentence the key selling point(s) that I'm looking for.

They'll say something like:

◊   Because it will save them money!

◊   Because it's great value

◊   Because there is nothing else available that's half as fast as this

◊   Because it will make them healthier

◊   ... And so on.

Of course I don't always get the answers I'm looking for. Often I'll get quite the opposite. I'll hear statements like:

◊   Because they'll be fools if they don't buy it

◊   Because it will give them peace of mind!

◊   Because it's what the market demands and they definitely need it.

◊   ... And so on.

These last are the kind of answers I dread to hear because, of course, their customers are not fools. And 'peace of mind' is a very intangible thing at the best of times. Likewise, if it's really what the market demands and consumers definitely need it, how come they aren't all already beating a path to our doors?

I'm also told that one of the really infuriating things about me is that if I don't get the 'right' answer the first time I ask my question, I usually ask the same question again. Us copywriters sometimes live very dangerous lives!

But it's only by asking questions like these that the principal selling points of your products or services become clear. For example, if you buy this product you will become healthier ... you'll save money ... your machinery will run faster, and so on.

And since I always find it most effective to work in 3s, I draw a pyramid with, what I consider to be, the three most important selling points that the client mentions. I then ask the client to tell me which one would they like me to put as number one at the top of 'the pyramid of importance', which is number two and which is number three?

For example, the client's 'pyramid of importance' for product X could be:

1. It'll save **YOU** money

2. **YOU**'ll find it great value   3. **YOU**'ll get nothing else in the
                                          market that's half as fast as this

Of course, the client may have many other selling points that he/she wants included but, at this stage, I always try to limit it to three. I then explain to the client that the reason I have limited it to three selling points is because I am now going to demonstrate what exactly happens to these three selling points when we present them to our readers in our sales letter. Effectively what happens is that the pyramid is turned sideways and it now represents the sound waves of the traditional street vendor selling his wares and trying to make the people passing by listen to, and pay attention to, his sales message.

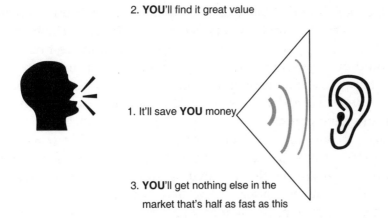

2. **YOU**'ll find it great value

1. It'll save **YOU** money

3. **YOU**'ll get nothing else in the
market that's half as fast as this

It's always the first selling point that sounds the loudest, gets the most attention and is remembered the longest. From then on, like sound waves rippling outwards, the selling points have less and less impact on the reader's eyes or ears. To take this to an extreme, imagine how much impact that a street vendor shouting out 15 or 20 selling points would have on passers by? Believe me, it would be very confusing indeed.

If you wish, therefore, to achieve maximum impact with your sales letter you need to carefully limit the number of selling points you require your reader to absorb and go for **maximum** impact with your best selling points. Make your number one selling point your USP ... your Unique Selling Point!

RULE 2: ADDRESS YOUR SALES MESSAGE TO THE RIGHT AUDIENCE

Many years ago, a long-established European firm, which specialises in selling garden bulbs and plants by mail order, decided to do a promotional mailing in Ireland. They knew exactly what they wanted to do. Furthermore, they knew exactly how to do it. They had many, many years' expertise in the mail order field. Their product catalogues were first-rate and their reputation for delivering top quality goods was second-to-none in many European countries, but not to the same extent in Ireland.

They had advertised their products from time to time in the Irish media, with a relatively high degree of success, and had decided that the time had come for them to try the direct mail approach to certain carefully-targeted areas in Ireland. Theirs was a fabulous *'Spring Garden'* offer. From them, for a modest outlay, you could purchase a bumper pack of top quality spring bulbs of every shape, size and description. And the sales promise was that, if you ordered immediately, next spring you could have the most beautiful spring garden in your entire neighbourhood.

Truly, it was an irresistible offer. The sales letter was a masterpiece and you simply couldn't take your eyes off the beautiful fresh spring flowers that featured in their brochure. They mailed out their offer and waited in great anticipation for the orders to come in. But within a few short days, they realised that something was terribly wrong. The number of orders that were coming in was nowhere near the level they were so confidently anticipating. They simply couldn't understand it. And, as the weeks went by, their very worse fears were confirmed; the mailing campaign was definitely not going to deliver the desired results.

What happened? Actually, it was an irate message returned in one of the pre-paid response envelopes by a recipient of the catalogue that gave them their first insight into what might be the cause of the problem. The message, in effect, said *'What's the point in offering me and all my neighbours an opportunity to have a beautiful spring garden when everybody in this area lives in high-rise apartment blocks with very small balconies?'*.

Uh Oh! It was the mailing list, and not the wonderful offer, that was at fault. A sizeable percentage of households on their mailing list had no garden at all! Whoever had supplied them with the mailing list had done them a considerable disservice!

The lesson to be learned from this is that you should always pay extra-careful attention to your mailing list. Because, if you have the wrong mailing list, no amount of magic in your sales letter will work for you. If you are mailing your sales letters into towns, cities or countries that you are not familiar with, it's definitely worth your while to make it your business to find someone who is familiar with these areas and ask their opinion about the area or people that you are planning to send your letter to.

Find out as much as you possibly can about the people and companies on the list before you even think about using it. If possible, get into your car and drive about the housing estates or the postal district areas that you are planning to mail into. Find out in advance as much as you possibly can about your target group.

This 'no garden' example reminds me of a wonderful story that is told about the pioneering door-to-door *Hoover* salesmen, who operated in the early days of the last century. These intrepid salesmen used to demonstrate the amazing cleaning powers of the Hoover by insisting on emptying a bag of dust and grit all over the anxious house-owners', and would-be purchasers', living room carpets. Generally speaking, the more the salesman scattered the dust on the carpet, and the more horrified the homeowner became, the more cheerful the salesman was.

And then, in a sublime moment of triumph, he would enquire of the house-owner where the electricity socket was. And without further ado, he would plug in the Hoover and the miracle machine would suck up all the dust in seconds! It must have been an astonishing performance to watch, and I'm told that it was on live demonstrations like these that the mighty *Hoover* empire was founded.

It was all so simple really and it worked so well, except for one poor salesman, who having cheerfully scattered the dust, despite the loud protestations of the anxious housewife, asked the vital question, *'Where's the electricity socket, Ma'am?'*, only to be informed, *'We sure don't have any electricity in this house and you sure are going to sweep up every bit of this mess in my living room this very instant'*.

I always chuckle when I'm reminded of that story, as it's an excellent example of what can go wrong if you don't address your sales message to the right audience. A simple little bit of pre-sales research would have revealed to the salesman that *'we sure don't have any electricity in this house'* and would have saved him the trouble of getting down on his knees and cleaning up his sales mess.

RULE 3: TRY TO AVOID THE DREADED 'DEAR SIR/MADAM' SALUTATION

How many times have you received sales letters in your mail that have greeted you with the timeworn salutation *'Dear Sir/Madam?'*. My guess is that, during your lifetime, you have received quite a number of letters that open like that. The sales message is either for Sir or for Madam!

Now let me ask you a question that always seems to get the male participants in my writing workshops decidedly uneasy. And my question to you is *'When did you last meet a madam?'*. For that matter, *'When did you last meet a sir?'*.

The answer to this question is *'probably never'*. That's why no really great sales letter today ever starts with this truly dreadful opening: *'Dear Sir/Madam'*. In my opinion, there is only one thing worse than a sales letter which starts with *'Dear Sir/Madam'* – it's the letter that goes to all the trouble of carefully personalising your address at the top of it and then goes on to say *'Dear Sir/Madam'*.

Any letter that has this mixture of careful personalisation followed with *'Dear Sir/Madam'* is either cheap, lazy, unimaginative or all three of these!

◊ **Cheap!** Because maybe it's a photocopied or pre-printed piece of paper upon which the address has been superimposed above the catchall *'Dear Sir/Madam'* salutation.

◊ **Lazy!** Because if it's not photocopied or pre-printed material, then all the indications are that the writer just couldn't be bothered investing a little bit of extra time working on his/her mail merge fields.

◊ **Unimaginative!** Because, in my opinion, there is nothing more uninspiring, old-fashioned and lack-lustre looking than the dreaded *'Dear Sir/Madam'* opening to a letter.

Time and time again, direct mail research reveals that a personalised letter with a personalised salutation generates a considerably higher response than a non-personalised *'Dear Sir/Madam'* letter.

Of course, I appreciate that you can't always, or you may not always want to, personalise your sales letters. For example, if you were doing a simple door-to-door letter drop in a neighbourhood, you wouldn't normally go to the extra cost and trouble of personalising them, because these are, in fact, cheaply produced pre-printed sales letters. But they don't have to look cheap! And they certainly don't need to have a weary yesteryear *'Dear Sir/Madam'* appearance.

Maybe, if you are sending out pre-printed letters in envelopes that have address labels affixed to them, you might be tempted to use the *'Dear Sir/Madam'* salutation on your letters. You might be tempted ... but please don't be! Because there are so many better, more interesting or more imaginative alternatives for you to select from – alternatives that will give your letter a more personal, or a more upbeat modern feel to it.

Here are a few alternatives that you might consider using but, before you even consider them, may I again emphasise to you that a personalised letter with the correct personalised salutation always pulls a better response than a non-personalised letter.

Alternative	When you might use it
Dear Customer	If your letters are going to existing customers
Dear Friend	Charity appeal letters sometimes opt for this opening as it saves them the cost of personalisation
Good Morning!	This is a bright and breezy salutation that I have used with great success
Great News!	Another cheery salutation, which has a far more upbeat tone to it than the dreaded *'Dear Sir/Madam'*
Hello!	I've used this successfully in a neighbourhood door-to-door mail drop when my letter is introducing a local service or supplier to householders
Hi!	A less formal version of *'Hello'*, which is frequently used on email sales letters.
	Nothing at all ... just a glorious blank. Sometimes, if your opening sentence is strong enough, your reader may not even notice that there is no salutation. What you need is an opening sentence along the lines of: *'Now I know you're not going to believe this ... but!'* or *'This is it! This is definitely the offer that you've been waiting for ... '*

RULE 4: MAKE YOUR LETTER'S APPEARANCE APPROPRIATE TO YOUR OFFER

Now, I want you to come with me for a pleasant little drive along a green country road in the lush farmlands of County Wexford, Ireland. And, as you are driving along humming *County Roads* or some such appropriate little song, you pass a farmyard and you see that Farmer A has put up a little wooden roadside sign which catches your eye. Here's Farmer A's sign:

A little bit further down the road you observe that Farmer A has some local competition. His neighbour, Farmer B, has a beautifully factory-produced sign up on the roadside advertising fresh eggs. Here's Farmer B's sign:

**Fresh Eggs
For Sale**

And you decide that it would be a nice idea, while you are in the country, to buy some farm fresh eggs to bring home with you. Which farmer do you think sells the freshest eggs: Farmer A, who has the rather rough-and-ready paint-daubed sign, or Farmer B, who has a perfectly-produced sign with the message presented in clear Times Roman lettering?

Most people would opt for Farmer A's eggs. You see, Farmer A's main business is obviously farming and he or his wife make some extra income by selling fresh eggs as a sideline to their main farm business. Farmer B, on the other hand, is obviously an entrepreneur whose business is selling eggs. He may not, in fact, be a farmer at all.

Now imagine, just imagine, that you normally do your weekly grocery shopping in two different supermarkets. In one supermarket, Farmer A's paint-daubed old wooden sign is on display at the ultra-modern refrigerated egg display cabinet. The other supermarket has Farmer B's crisp professionally-produced sign at the refrigerated display cabinet. Which supermarket would you buy your eggs from?

Most people would immediately opt to buy their eggs from the supermarket that has the crisp professionally-produced sign. In fact, many customers might complain to the management if they were presented with a rough-and-ready-looking paint-daubed wooden sign in a modern supermarket.

It's all a matter of putting the correct appearance on your offer. In a supermarket, buyers want to buy supermarket fresh eggs, so they look for the supermarket egg sign. In the country. people buying directly from the farmer want to buy authentic farm-fresh eggs, so they look for the sign that suggests a real farm.

Always try and see your sales letter and your offer through your readers' eyes. Be careful about using coloured paper or different coloured print, or unusual type fonts, if you think that your target audience may react negatively to them. Remember the simple rule *'Always put yourself in your reader's place'*. This is not to say that you have to kill creativity and colour entirely. All I'm saying to you is *'play safe'*! Try and anticipate what your reader expects from you, and give them exactly what they are looking for.

Some years ago I read in a marketing magazine about an American retail store, which attributed its marketing success to the very distinctive yellow paper that they used, in all their sales and promotional letters. I thought no more about it, until a client of mine in the retail business in Ireland rang me to tell me that he had heard about this *'yellow wow!'* at a direct marketing convention that he had just attended. He wanted to know what my feelings were about him trying it out in Ireland. I told him about the US article that I had read and I went on to explain to him that I really didn't know what would happen if he tried using yellow company paper with an Irish target group. After much discussion, we decided to take the risk and give 'yellow' a go.

The outcome was ... well, it *was* a success, not a huge success, but it definitely pulled in a good response. At the end of the day, our gut feeling was that the novelty factor associated with using yellow paper had a definite part to play in the enhanced response level. We both agreed that the experiment was worthwhile, but rather than switch all future sales letters to yellow paper, we decided that we would keep yellow in our promotional toolbox and use it from time to time as a novelty.

That adds up to two retail stores in two different continents that have found that yellow can work for them, but a novel approach like this may not work for everyone. For example, can you imagine what your reaction would be if your local bank manager started communicating with you on bright yellow paper? Something tells me that this just wouldn't work very well for a bank, but I'm wide open to be proven wrong on this.

But do try to make the appearance of your letter appropriate to your offer.

RULE 5: QUICKLY ANSWER THE WI-IFM QUESTION FOR YOUR READER

What's in it for me? (WI-IFM). We discussed this at an earlier stage in this book. If you recall, WI-IFM is the radio frequency that everybody is tuned into 24 hours a day, every single day of the year. It plays such an important part in the success of your sales letter that it's worthwhile having another little look at how it operates. What would your immediate reaction be if you received a letter in the post that opened as follows?

Dear Sir/Madam

With assets of over 50 Billion and employing in excess of 5,000 employees in more than 20 locations world-wide, each with a specific target aim and commitment to meet the emerging global demand for the key resources and inter-active energies that our company founders had in ...

Isn't this a truly dreadful way to start a sales letter? It opens with the dreaded *'Dear Sir/Madam'*. It then proceeds to waffle on about how big and important the company that's sending you this letter is. Furthermore, the opening sentence is far too long. But what kills this sales letter entirely from the readers' perspective is that the reader simply doesn't get a look in. The company is so busy talking 'big company speak' in its opening paragraph that it fails entirely to answer the WI-IFM question for the reader.

A very persuasive sales letter must tell me quickly and tell me clearly *'what's in it for me?'*, if it's to lure me successfully on to reading the rest of it.

RULE 6: KISS (KEEP IT SIMPLE, STUPID!)

Once upon a time, and it wasn't so very long ago either, I was invited to visit a company website. So I duly went online and, on the home page of the site, I found myself presented with the following mind-boggling choice of actions:

Click here for background company information	Click here for an introduction to our company
Click here for our company history	Click here for statistical details about our company
Click here for Company Impro/R	Click here for further information

Wow! Which one would you click on? To this day I have never discovered what *'Company Impro/R'* is and I don't think that I will ever bother finding out. What's happening here is that some 'techie' has gone into information-overload mode and has presented the reader with far too many different and confusing action choices. The effect is frightening, because unless you have a huge amount of idle time on your hands, you are going to go elsewhere when you are presented with a choice like this. How much easier and more inviting it would have been if there was just this one simple 'KISS'-style button to press.

One important 'KISS' area that you should keep a careful watch on is pricing and VAT. For example, I sometimes receive sales letters that tell me, in effect, that: *'All it costs is €199 plus VAT at the standard rate'*.

Now quickly – very quickly – can you tell me which of the following options represents the **VAT-inclusive** price of the above commodity or service on offer **to you**?

◊   **Option 1:** €218.90

◊   **Option 2:** €240.79

◊   **Option 3:** €199.00

I guess that you probably haven't got the mental energy to even bother working out which of the above options is the correct answer to my question. In any case, the right answer could be any of the above options, depending on whether the product or service on offer attracts VAT at a rate of 13.5%, 21% or 0%. You should always do the VAT calculations for your reader, because if you don't, the danger is that they mightn't do it for themselves. And, if they don't know the all-in price of your product/service, at best, it might cause disappointment later or, at worst, they won't buy it.

Also you should always keep your eyes open for little ambiguities or mind-twisters like this that might creep into your sales letters: *'Cheques made payable to the addressee are not acceptable'*.

Here's another example of a priceless mind-twister that I came across not so very long ago.

> The amount you pay is the total of 'A & B' (if applicable) plus p&p (see table 2 for the appropriate p&p). Add 'C' to the amount of 'A' if 'B' is not applicable. Local taxes also apply.

I guess 'priceless' is the correct word for me to use in this situation. Because, no matter what way I looked at it, I found it impossible to calculate the price because I hadn't a breeze what the local taxes were.

RULE 7: MAKE IT EASY FOR YOUR READER TO RESPOND TO YOU

This rule sounds obvious, doesn't it? Well, you'd be surprised at how many companies ignore, or overlook, it. How many times have you read a wonderful sales letter, the product or the service on offer looks good, the price is right? It's all so interesting and you definitely want to find out more? So you grab the phone and look down at the bottom of the letter to establish whom to contact only to find something like this:

> '... Please don't hesitate to contact us if you need more information'.

Yikes! Who exactly are you going to contact? Who is 'us'? Let's say it's a large company that employs over 500 people that is making you this interesting offer. Is this letter really asking you to contact all 500 employees? Okay, I'm exaggerating! But I'm always surprised at how often I come across the expression *'please don't hesitate to contact us'* at the bottom of what is otherwise an excellent sales letter.

The reason why I don't like this line is because it immediately puts an obstacle between the reader and the person/company that he or she is trying to contact. Effectively, it means that your reader has to pick up the telephone and shuffle around trying to explain himself to the switchboard operator who answers his call. Instead of simply saying *'Hello, may I speak to Mary Browne in your Sales Department please?',* the reader is reduced to saying something along the lines of *'Hello, I'm ringing about a letter which I received from your company in connection with a special offer you are making on "whatever", I'm not sure who I should talk to but can you ... blah blah blah'.*

Sometimes, when you make 'blah blah' calls like this, everything does, in fact, run smoothly and in no time at all you are put through to a pleasant person who knows exactly what you are enquiring about. Sometimes!

But I guess I must have been born under an unlucky Tel-star because I always seem to get the switchboard operator who asks me ... *'What letter?'* ... *'What offer?'* ... *'What exactly is this in connection with?'*.... and so on and so forth. And I always feel unwanted from the outset.

Now, of course, I understand the reason why companies put those catchall invitations *'please don't hesitate to contact us'* on their sales letters. It's because they fear that if they put a identifiable contact name on the letter the named person may be inundated with calls or, worse still, the person may be out sick or have left the company or whatever when you call. And while all of this is very sound logic from the company's viewpoint, that's exactly what it is .... *'logical from the company's viewpoint'.*

A writer of a very persuasive sales letter always puts him or herself in the readers' place and makes it as easy as possible for the readers to respond to the offer. Wherever possible, you should clearly identify a named person for your readers to contact. Clients sometimes tell me that this is not always possible or, indeed, feasible, because they have a full telesales team standing by to take incoming calls. Sometimes, the individual members of these teams operate on a commission-only payment basis and I'm told that there would be an outright war if one person were singled out in a promotional mailing to receive the bulk of incoming calls.

If this is the situation, I always tell them to consider using a uniform name approach.

A uniform name approach works like this: everybody in the telesales team is given the name *'Caroline'* or some such. Of course, they hold on to their surname for commission identification purposes. So you have a Caroline O'Reagan, Caroline Smith, Caroline McCoy and so on. This allows the company to use the uniform name *'Caroline'* on all its advertising material and sales letters. And when a potential customer contacts the switchboard asking to speak to Caroline, they are immediately identified as someone who is looking for a quotation. And without further ado, they are passed to a *'Caroline'*, who can help them.

While I'm on the subject of telephone responses, can I mention here that a FreePhone response number or a *'cost of a local call only from anywhere in the country'* telephone response number definitely does increase response levels, particularly if your sales letter is addressed to homes rather than businesses.

Likewise, Freepost reply and prepaid business reply envelopes also make it easy for your readers to respond to your sales message. Personally, I prefer using Freepost reply, as opposed to the more traditional licensed Business Reply envelopes. The reason for this, of course, is because **free** is one of the magic words and I tend to prefer anything that has a magic word association with it.

Clients sometimes question the benefit of paying the extra cost of including a Freepost reply envelope with their sales letters. In this day and age of speedy fax and email communications, you could be tempted to trim costs by leaving out the Freepost reply envelope option entirely. My advice to you is don't be tempted to leave it out, because you'd be surprised at how many people still prefer to use this option, especially if confidential personal information like date of birth, or credit card details are required.

There is no question about it but the more reply options you give your reader, the more replies you will get to your communications. This is particularly true of a fax reply option. In recent years, I have been encouraging all my clients to include a full A4 size fax response sheet in all their mailings and this additional sheet of paper has definitely earned its keep. By the way, the reason why I insist on using a full A4 sheet of paper is because A4 is the most paper-friendly size for stand-alone fax machines to accommodate.

In summary, therefore, you should give your reader the widest possible choice of reply options, which includes:

◊　A named person to respond to

◊　A specific telephone number – preferably free or subsidised to the extent that it costs no more than the cost of a local call

◊　A fax reply number which, preferably, is also free or subsidised

◊　An email reply address

◊　A Freepost or pre-paid business reply envelope and

◊　An address to call into, if they wish.

SUMMARY OF CHAPTER 22
HERE'S WHAT YOU SAY AND HOW YOU SAY IT

☐ Know your selling points. The clearer your selling points are, the more effective your sales letter will be. Present your 'Unique Selling Point' (USP) to your reader as early as possible in your sales letter.

☐ Address your message to the right audience – even the best of sales letters will not work, if they are addressed to the wrong people.

☐ Try to avoid using the dreaded *'Dear Sir/Madam'* salutation at the top of your sales letters. Not only is this kind of salutation a giveaway sign that the same letter is being sent to every Tom, Dick, or Jane but it also conveys old-fashioned and negative vibes about your company.

☐ Make the appearance of your letter appropriate to your offer.

☐ Quickly answer the 'WI-IFM?' (What's in it for me?) question for your reader in your sales letter.

☐ Remember KISS! (Keep it simple, stupid.)

☐ Make it easy for your readers to respond to your sales letter. The more response options you give them, the more you increase your chances of getting responses.

23. NEVER SELL TO A STRANGER

> **The Caterpillar and Alice looked at each other for some time in silence; at last the Caterpillar took the hookah out of its mouth, and addressed her in a languid, sleepy voice. 'Who are you?' said the Caterpillar.**
> Lewis Carroll, *Alice's Adventures in Wonderland* (1865), Ch.5.

'Never Sell to a Stranger'. That's a good catchy headline, and it's the bedrock upon which a very successful and sophisticated marketing communication strategy called CRM is built.

I have to confess that, the first time I was introduced to the concept of 'never sell to a stranger', it puzzled me greatly because my immediate reaction was *'How on earth are most of us going to make money if we're only prepared to sell our products or services to people we know?'*.

But like all catchy headlines, it's the CRM success story behind the headline, rather than the headline itself that is worth looking into. But what exactly does CRM stand for?

To some, CRM stands for Customer Relationship **Marketing**, while for others CRM stands for Customer Relationship **Management**. The truth is that CRM is probably a mixture of both management and marketing techniques.

One of the best ways to understand how the mechanisms of CRM work is to picture your business as a bathtub, into which hot water is constantly being poured through a tap at one end and disappearing down the drain at the other end. This bathtub is where all the selling activity in your company takes place, orders are received, prices are calculated, stocks are despatched and so on and so forth.

The hot water pouring into your bathtub represents the flow of customers who do business with you. Each time you advertise, or send out sales letters or special offers in the mail, you increase the flow of hot water into your bathtub. And then, as time goes by, and your customers begin to forget your advertising message and sales letters, the flow of hot water gradually slows down until, eventually, it becomes no more than a trickle.

In many ways, the ebb and flow of the water into your bathtub is quite typical of the sales cycles of many businesses. Business flows fast and slow, while customers come and ... GO!

Hold on now! Wait a minute. Customers come and ... GO! But, of course they don't go forever, they come back and do more business in due course, don't they? I guess the answer to this last question is: some do and some don't. Some are so loyal to you that they will always want to come back. Some are lazy and will only come back to you because or when they haven't the energy to go elsewhere.

But then there are the customers who don't come back. Ever! And there's all kind of reasons for this. Reasons like: maybe they have no further need for your product or service, perhaps a competitor has befriended them; or your competitor's prices are cheaper. It could be that your competitor is more conveniently located to them and gives them a better service, or whatever. Some customers, over time, may just drift away from you for no particular reason at all and you lose contact with them. They just disappear down the drain, as it were, because your bathtub has no plug in it to stop them going.

Now, imagine what would happen if you inserted a plug in your bathtub. The moment you put in this plug, the hot water pouring into it ceases to disappear down the drain and your bathtub begins to fill up. Effectively, this is what happens when you begin to collect the names and addresses of the people who do business with you. You create a 'database plug', which acts in the very same way as a real plug and your bathtub begins to fill up with hot water. Or, to put it another way; your database begins to fill up with valuable names and addresses of customers that you can contact whenever you wish.

Actually, there is nothing new about the concept of holding on to names and addresses of customers and keeping in contact with them by sending them promotional material from time to time. Catalogue companies, mail order companies and department stores have been doing this for generations. But with the arrival of the word processors and the PC in the 1970s and 1980s came the dawn of a new era of mass personalised mailings and a new marketing buzzword was born: 'database marketing'.

Those were simple days, when things like a personalised sales letter could impress your customers greatly. And those were the days when *'Volume was King!'*. Everybody in the direct mail business talked about volume, and was looking for new and quicker ways to produce vast quantities of personalised letters.

It was a time when I can recall the managing director of a company that I then worked with, heading off to catch a flight to an important business meeting – an exploratory meeting to find out more about an awesome new printing machine that created individually personalised sales letters in seconds. It was called a 'laser printer' and, on his return, he proudly quoted to us the immortal words used by American journalist, Lincoln Steffens after his visit to the Soviet Union in 1919: *'I have seen the future and it works'.*

But the ability to inundate the market with flawlessly-produced personalised sales letters didn't quite work out the way those early database-marketing pioneers predicted.

Soon, very soon, consumers began to tire of this new personalised bulk-mailing fad. The novelty of seeing your name on a letter – sometimes repeated three or four times in a single page – began to wear off, as the market got tired of the increasing amount of personalised mail that was clogging up letterboxes. In many ways, you can't really blame them. Because much of what arrived in the letterboxes was just a repeat of the personalised message that had come though the month before, and the month before that again.

Inevitably, things began to get tougher for direct marketers, as customers began to demand that their names be taken off mailing lists and these demands were reinforced with the statutory powers of newly-emerging data protection legislation. As consumers increasingly demanded more data-protection legislation, the very future of database-driven direct marketing campaigns was threatened.

Something had to be done, and out of this consumer-hostile environment emerged a new, more customer-friendly, approach to database marketing called **Customer Relationship Marketing,** or CRM for short.

Instead of bombarding your customers with unsolicited mail pieces containing offers that they may not want, the new CRM approach centred on building positive relationships with your customers, getting to know them better and treating them like valued friends rather than strangers. Now you can see where my catchy headline comes from ... *'never sell to a stranger'.*

To understand how CRM works, you first need to appreciate the power of the follow-up sales letter.

For decades, direct marketers have known that, if you send out unsolicited sales information to people whom you don't know, your chances of getting a big response to your mailing are not as good as they would be if you sent the material to people who know you.

That's why so many direct mail experts all over the world recommend that when you send out a sales letter to people whom you don't know (a 'cold' mailing), you should always try to send out a follow-up reminder letter approximately 10 to 15 days after you have sent your first introductory mailing. The reason for this is twofold: not only does your follow-up letter act as a useful reminder to the recipient of the availability of your product or service in the marketplace, but it also helps to reinforce the personal link between you and your readers.

First time around your readers may not know you. You are, in effect, a complete stranger to them and the corollary of this holds true as well, they may be strangers to you. But, by the time, your second follow-up letter arrives, there is a good possibility that they will recall that you have been in contact with them in recent weeks, so you won't be quite the same stranger to them that you were when your first letter arrived, especially if you make a point of reminding them in your follow-up letter that you've been in touch with them before. For example:

Dear Mr Hayes-McCoy

You may recall that I wrote to you at the beginning of the month to tell you about the arrival of super-product-plus in your area. At that time, I mentioned to you that this is one of the most … etc, etc, etc.

The problem, of course, with sending out a follow-up reminder letter like this to a stranger is that, if the recipient is definitely not in the market for your product or service, it could be a complete waste of time, effort and money. In fact, it could instantly be categorised by the recipient as being 'junk mail' and this could be very dangerous for your business, especially if you are selling a specialised product or service to a strictly limited market.

For example, if you are selling:

◊   Church candles to parish priests

◊   Legal stationary to legal firms

◊   Fine wines to wine connoisseurs

◊   Deep-sea diving equipment to deep-sea divers

◊   … And so on.

It's in cases like this, where you have a clearly-defined, and possibly very limited, market, that the principle of *'never sell to a stranger'* can have a crucial impact on the success of your business. Because, although you may not know these people personally, they represent the core market group into which you **must** sell your products or services, otherwise your business will not survive. This is a very valuable group to you and you certainly can't afford to take the risk of alienating them by inundating them with what they perceive to be junk mail.

That's why it's so important for you to, right from the outset, to cultivate these people and, if possible, make them your friends. Because, by making these people your friends, not only are you creating a more positive environment in which to sell your products and services to them, but you are also making it more difficult for your competitors to sell their products to them.

In your initial sales letters to these people, you must work hard at building up a good relationship with them. And once you have established this, you must cultivate their fledgling friendship very carefully. Remember the advice that old Polonius in *Hamlet* gave to his son:

> 'The friends thou hast, and their adoption tried,
> Grapple them to thy soul with hoops of steel.'
> Shakespeare, *Hamlet* (1601), Act 1, sc 3, 1. 59.

Presented like this it all sounds so easy, doesn't it? All you have to do is build up a carefully selected reservoir of friends – keep in touch with them, cultivate friendships and then sit back and watch your sales pour in. Actually, it's not easy. It's far more difficult than you might think. It's difficult because:

◊ You need to decide **where to start** – what list of 'strangers' will you concentrate your energies on to try and turn them into friends?

◊ You need to settle on **how often** you will communicate with your target group and what exactly you will communicate to them.

◊ You need to make a decision about **how long** will you keep a person's name on your list if, despite your best communication efforts, he or she doesn't buy anything from you.

◊ You need to fix on **who is responsible** for looking after your reservoir of friends and making sure that the water in it is always clean (your list is constantly updated and refined) and that a warm friendly friendship temperature is always maintained. Remember, you don't just want your bathtub to fill up with hot water; you also need to make sure that the water in your bathtub is never allowed to go cold. In other words, you need to keep the relationships warm by keeping in touch with your customers on a regular basis.

WHERE DO YOU START?

In some businesses, your starting point is obvious. For example, if you plan to sell candles to parish priests, then clearly your initial target group is parish priests. A mailing list of these is readily available to rent or buy from most mailing list brokers. If you look up the Yellow Pages, or an online search engine like Google, you should quickly be able to identify mailing list brokers in your area.

Sometimes your target group may not be so clearly defined. For example, you may plan to sell motorcars to companies that have a fleet of 10 or more company cars. In this situation, it might be difficult for you to decide to whom to address your sales letter. In circumstances like this, a reputable mailing list broker can give you invaluable advice and assistance in helping you to pinpoint the most likely mailing list.

But no matter where you get your initial list from you should always try and choose the target group of 'strangers that you want to befriend' carefully, so that you don't waste time and money trying to make friends with the wrong people. That's why an outdated list or a list that has been carelessly assembled should be avoided at all costs. A good mailing list broker will be able to advise you about all these matters.

When you are building up your mailing list, you must take great care to ensure that all the information and address details, etc, on it is are as correct and as up-to-date as you can possibly make it. Once you have the best possible mailing list to hand, no matter how small it is, you have a target group to receive your sales letter … or two or three or more sales letters.

HOW OFTEN?

To answer this, let me ask you a simple question: *'What do you call someone who you enjoy meeting for a drink every Friday evening after work?'*.

Every Friday evening, without fail, you meet this person and you discuss the events of the week and you share jokes and experiences. What do you call this special person? The answer to this question is: 'a friend'.

Okay, you've got a friend. But what would you call this person if, every time you met him or her for a drink after work on Friday evening, they asked you for the loan of €20? That's right! Every Friday evening, without fail, they ask you for a loan of money.

Now there's all kind of answers to this question of mine and the chances are that none of them would be very friendly or complimentary. But, inevitably, what I suspect would happen in circumstances like these is that, very soon, you would get absolutely fed up with always being 'touched' for a loan each Friday evening and in no time at all you would stop meeting this very demanding friend of yours.

Now, let's do a little quantum leap and apply this behavioural pattern to someone who receives a very persuasive sales letter from you carefully explaining the benefits and virtues of your products or services and asking them to do business with you. First time around, your letter will make the desired impact and they will read it with interest. Depending on their requirement for your product or service they might even buy from you immediately. Alternatively, if they have no immediate need for your product or service, they might do nothing more than make a note of your company's name for future contact.

But let's suppose that, a month later, they receive **the very same letter** from you again asking them to do business with you. What happens then? Well, they might glance over it again, they may even buy something from you, but there's no question about it, this second repeat letter won't have the same impact on them as your first sales letter. But keep going, if you continue to mail them this very same sales letter month after month asking them to do business with you, what happens then?

What happens is that, in time, they won't even bother opening the envelope in which your sales letter arrives. They'll take one look at the outer envelope and they'll discard it on the basis that they know exactly what your sales letter inside is going to ask them to do. It all sounds so familiar doesn't it?

It's a bit like that Friday night drinking-companion pattern that I've mentioned above, where the requests for a loan of money become so predictable that, after a while, you stop meeting your friend for a drink. The same thing happens with predictable sales letters: the pattern becomes monotonous. The letter writer has fallen into the trap of concentrating too much on selling: 'the trap of concentrating too much on selling!' What does this mean? How can you possibly oversell? It means that: **sometimes we are all so busy selling our products and services that we forget that we are buyers too!** And what we have to buy here is one of the most important things of all; we have to buy our customers' friendship and loyalty.

We have to buy our customers' friendship and loyalty?

Yes! Furthermore, if we keep on sending our customers and potential customers, the same sales letter with the same request to do business, we are certainly not – not at all – buying their friendship and loyalty. All we are doing is running the risk of being a bore! To avoid this happening, we need to liven things up and enhance our relationships with our customers by making all our sales letters interesting, informative and possibly ... **unpredictable.**

Imagination, innovation, creativity and unpredictability are some of the most effective tools in your CRM toolbox. Of these, 'unpredictability' is the greatest tool of all. By this I mean, if you're planning to keep in touch on a regular basis with your carefully selected target group of customers and friends, you need to spice up your sales letters by making them unpredictable and interesting. And one sure-proof way of making a sales letter unpredictable is not to sell anything at all in it! From time to time along the way, use your sales letter to **'buy'** a little friendship instead.

Occasionally, send your customers and would-be customers an 'unnecessary letter.' For example, write to them from time to time and wish them well and tell them that you value their friendship and custom. Send them birthday cards, St. Valentine's Day cards or something that you think they'll enjoy. You'll be amazed at how much friendship a cheerful 'unnecessary' letter will buy for you. And believe me, that friendship will, in time, result in increased business for you.

People sometimes ask me *'But what kind of an unnecessary letter can I use in my business?'*. And, of course, I know what they are thinking. They are thinking to themselves that it's all very well for oddball copywriters like me to send my clients and friends 'unnecessary' letters. But what do you do if, for example, you are an eminent solicitor or a very respectable finance company? In a scenario like this, the unsaid question that is being so politely put to me is: *'Surely I don't expect the likes of eminent solicitors or respectable finance companies to send out unnecessary "buy friendship" letters to their customers and potential customers?'*. The short answer is *'Of course, I do. Why not? Everybody needs friends'*.

But what kind of 'unnecessary' letters can we send them?

Let's pretend that we want to send a careful mix of 'buying-friendship' letters to all our customers and friends every single month of the year. Now remember, we're only pretending. I'm emphasising this last point to you because it would be neither practical nor profitable for you to mail out 'buying-friendship' letters all the time. You need to mix them with hard no-nonsense sales letters as well. Remember, a really effective CRM strategy strikes a careful balance between the buying and the selling process. But, for the purpose of this 'let's pretend' exercise, here is a month-by-month calendar of top-of-the-head ideas and suggestions for 'unnecessary' letters, together with some of my favourite monthly examples.

Month: **January**
Event: **New Year**
Strategy: Send out a personalised letter wishing all your customers and friends a very happy New Year. Tell them that you are looking forward to being of service to them in the coming year and remind them that, if they have any suggestions to make to you about how you can improve your service to them, you'd welcome hearing from them.

My favourite: I received a letter from my financial advisor and it had one of those 'one-page-a-day' calendars attached to it (you know the ones which have a little worldly quotation or an uplifting thought for the day at the bottom of each tear-off page?) And the accompanying sales letter told me: *'Happy New Year, Robert. The enclosed calendar is a little gift for you. By the way, I've torn off the page for 15 January and attached it to this letter because that's the day I'd like to meet you and bring you up to date, etc, etc, etc.'* (Okay this is both buying and selling, but I did enjoy receiving it and, of course, I used the calendar.)

Month: February
Event: St. Valentine's Day
Strategy: Send a simple letter or a card to your customers
                  saying *'Happy St. Valentine's Day. We LOVE doing
                  business with you'*.
My favourite: I received an invitation to a party with an
                  accompanying letter signed by every employee in
                  the company telling me: *'We'd **all** love you to join us
                  for our special party'*. (Nice touch that, I really felt
                  wanted.)

Month: March
Event: St. Patrick's Day
Strategy: Send your customers and friends a letter wishing
                  them the very best for St Patrick's Day.
My favourite: I got an unusual letter from a client company of
                  mine, written by St. Patrick's snake. It was fun
                  because, as all good Irish people know, St. Patrick
                  is reputed to have banished snakes from Ireland
                  forever! But this letter, which incidentally was
                  written in very "snaky" handwriting, assured me
                  that this was not so, and that this snake had been
                  quietly working away in XYD company for ages.
                  The snake went on to explain that it was no
                  ordinary snake – it was a friendly adder!
                  Furthermore, it had done a very **"friendly adder's
                  job"** on all the company's products for St. Patrick's
                  week – it had actually marked down all prices by
                  25%. So now was the time for me to get a real
                  bargain.

Month: April
Event: Summer Time in Ireland arrives and the clocks go
                  forward an hour.
Strategy: Write to all your customers and friends and tell
                  them that the clocks will be going forward next
                  Sunday. They will be getting up earlier, which will
                  give them all the more time to enjoy the enclosed
                  special offer or whatever.

My favourite: I received a little note from a local store telling me that, because I was getting up early next Sunday there would be a free, freshly cut bunch of daffodils awaiting me there, if I simply presented my letter to the shop assistant before 11am that day.

Month: May
Event: Mayday!
Strategy: Write to your customers and tell them that you are expecting a huge new delivery of stocks and that you are having a massive 'invitation only' May Day Sale to make room in your warehouse for your new stock. And, of course they are invited.

My favourite: I received a letter enclosing an untied 'May Day' bow tie. I was informed that it's always useful in an emergency to know how to tie a bow tie. And if I didn't know how to tie the enclosed bow tie, I was to telephone this number and someone would come out and teach me how to do it immediately. I was also informed that... *'Oh! By the way, while we are out with you we'd like to tell you more about how to 'tie up' a better pension plan as well'.* (Okay, there's buying and selling in here too, but I enjoyed the bow tie.)

Month: June
Event: Mid-summer day, Mid-summer madness!
Strategy: Write and tell all your customers and friends that at this time of the year you always like to have a Mid-Summer Madness Sale. And when they see your rock-bottom bargain prices, they'll understand why it's call Mid-Summer Madness!

My favourite: A note delivered early one beautiful sunny Saturday morning in June, saying just that ... *'Isn't it a beautiful sunny mid-summer Saturday morning! Don't waste a moment of it, come on out and have lunch in the garden in your local Hotel which is serving sumptuous mid-summer lunches at unbeatable mid-summer madness prices'.*

Month:	July
Event:	Picnic time!
Strategy:	Organise a picnic to somewhere interesting. Include a treasure hunt and a barbecue and fun and games for the children. Write and tell your customers all about it and invite them to come along with their kids.
My favourite:	I received a letter from a car dealer telling me that they had a special *'July & August holiday emergency car kit'* available for customers who were planning on bringing their cars to the continent. The kit included all sorts of useful things like spare fuses, bulbs, maps, an emergency breakdown triangle sign, tow rope, torch, First Aid kit, punctured tyre inflator and so on. And I was told that I was welcome to borrow one of these kits 'free of charge' for the duration of my holiday. Naturally I was expected to return the borrowed kit on my return from holidays.

Month:	August
Event:	Summer holiday time!
Strategy:	Send your customers and friends an exotic postcard from foreign parts. Tell them you are on holidays but you are thinking about them and would like to wish them well and that you'll be back in the office on the xth of the month if they need you. Inform them that they can still contact you by mobile phone, if they need you urgently.
My favourite:	A short letter from foreign parts that appeared to be written in Greek. And I was told (in the English opening paragraph) that if I wanted to understand Greek instantly all I had to do was hold this letter up to a mirror. And it really did work! I've no idea how long it took the company to do it, but by carefully typing every word backwards, they had created a simple short letter which at first glance looked and read like Greek but when you held it

up to a mirror you were greeted with a cheerful sales message in English. Something like:

!⊤ЯƎdoЯ ⅃⅃Ǝɯ ƎЯA UOY ƎqOH (Hope you are well, Robert! – Incidentally, I created this Greek-looking sentence by using some of the symbols in my Word programme.)

Month:	September
Event:	Back-to-School time
Strategy:	Write to all your customers and friends and tell them about something fascinating which you've been studying up on because … **it's back to school time**. For example: Tell them the origins of why motor cars in Ireland and Britain drive on the left hand side of the road? Alternatively, tell them that a chap called Dunlop invented the pneumatic tyre in Belfast, or something else of this fascinating ilk. You'd be surprised at the large number of people who enjoy receiving interesting (and possibly useless) pieces of information like this.
My favourite:	A letter telling me it was back-to-school time and pointing out that some of the things we got up to in our own school days were actually good fun. Like, how we used to spend hours making invisible ink … and the PS of the letter, which I was informed contained a very special message for me, was written in just that... 'invisible ink'! You actually had to warm up the letter to read the secret message. (Okay, it was real *Boy's Own* stuff, but it was fun. They used lemon juice for the invisible ink.)

Month:	October
Event:	Clocks go back an hour
Strategy:	Write and tell your customers that the clocks have gone back and they have just saved an hour in their lives. Ask them *'Can I have that hour?'* And invite them to join you for coffee for an hour to discuss how you can serve them better in the future.

My favourite: I received a letter accompanied with a mini
Cadbury's chocolate *Time Out* bar. And I was told
that with the clocks going back I now had an ideal
opportunity to take some delicious 'Time-Out' and
... so on and so forth.

Month:	November
Event:	Bleakest month of the year!
Strategy:	Cheer up all your customers and friends by telling them that you've decided to do something special to help them get rid of those **Bleak November Blues!**

My favourite: A letter accompanied with a very simple little book
of jokes and witticisms (two A4 Sheets folded down
and stapled together) to cheer me up in bleak
November. The book was very obviously in-
company-made and I was told that all the company
staff had been asked to contribute their favourite
joke or funny story to it. It was very cheerful
mailing to receive on a miserable wet November
morning.

Month:	December
Event:	Happy Christmas
Strategy:	Send all your customers and friends a special *'Happy Christmas'* letter instead of a run-of-the-mill Christmas greeting card. It will certainly make you stand out from the crowd and it gives you the space to thank them for their custom and friendship over the year.

My favourite: It was many years ago, but I still have it. I got a
wonderful press-out Christmas card from Judith
Donovan (the *Queen* of direct marketing). When
you pressed out various bits and pieces of the card,
it turned into an old-style mantelpiece made out of
cardboard, complete with miniature Christmas
cards on top and Christmas stockings hanging
down. Everything was cleverly designed to place
over your computer monitor and effectively turned

it into a fireplace. And Judith also enclosed a
floppy disk for me to pop into my disk drive and
immediately my computer monitor featured a rich,
warm, glowing fire with a Yuletide log burning
merrily away in it. It looked wonderful and it was
great to come back to my office and see a cheerful
fire blazing away in my computer screen-
mantelpiece.

There you have it! There you have a list of 12 possible monthly
reasons for mailings that I have picked at random and shared
with you. But the reasons for mailing don't have to be selected at
random. Don't forget that the best CRM programmes are
interactive programmes, where two-way communication between
you and your target group is actively encouraged. So, if you
simply ask your target group from time to time what kind of
mailings they would like to receive from you, you could learn
some great ideas from them. And, oh! By the way, don't forget to
say *'Thank you'* from time to time to your customers and friends.
Everybody likes to get a *'Thank you'* letter. That's why I'd like to
devote the next chapter of my book to *'Thank you'*.

SUMMARY OF CHAPTER 23:
HERE'S WHAT YOU SAY AND HOW YOU SAY IT

☐ Remember, your customers are human. If you keep on sending
them the same sales letters, eventually they will stop reading
them entirely.

☐ Sometimes we are all so busy concentrating on selling our
services that we forget that we are 'buyers' too! And what we
have to buy is one of the most important things of all:
Friendship!

☐ It's worth your while, particularly if your customer target group
is strictly limited in number, and there is a danger that you will
bore them to death with repetitive sales letters, to send them
'unnecessary' or 'friendship' letters from time to time.

☐ Introduce 'unpredictability' into your customer communications,
this adds enjoyment and spice to your sales letters and makes

them more memorable. It also gives you a reason for keeping in touch with your customer target group on a regular basis.

☐ Remember, the reason why it's so important for you to keep in touch with your customers on a regular basis is because you want to keep your name 'up-front' in their minds when the time comes for them to buy.

☐ Because if you don't keep your name 'up-front' in your customers' and potential customers' minds, your competitors might steal a march on you by being in the right place at the right time ... when the actual buying decision is made.

24. 'THANK YOU' SALES LETTERS

'Curtsey while you are thinking what to say.
It saves time.'
Lewis Carroll, *Through the Looking Glass* (1872), Ch.2.

'Thank you' letters are a very important part of the sales process. And it always surprises me how few companies and organisations use them to maximum effect. Most of the *'Thank you'* letters that I have seen over the years are little more than receipts and far too many of them fall into the dreaded *'Dear Sir/Madam'* salutation category. This always surprises me because I can think of no better way of 'buying friendship' that a nicely worded and carefully presented *'Thank you'* letter.

Generally speaking, I find that charities invest more time and money in sending out *'Thank you'* letters than most commercial companies do. The reasons why they do it is to acknowledge receipt of a donation from a generous benefactor **and** to strengthen the bond between the benefactor and the charitable agency. You see, most charities have long ago discovered that, the more often they keep in touch with their donors, the more committed these people become to the objectives of the charity.

I always find it strange that more shops, businesses, banks, supermarkets etc don't send out more *'Thank you'* letters to their own customers. After all, surely the same customer loyalty strategy should work as well for businesses as it does for charities.

What I'm talking about here is plain, simple, one-to-one communication 'Thank you' letters' that are not accompanied with discount coupons or money-saving vouchers etc. I'm talking about the kind of 'Thank you' letter that you would get from a friend.

Let me give you an example of a very 'good to receive' 'Thank you' letter that was sent out by a charity agency called Refugee Trust International.

Refugee Trust International is a small charity agent, operating out of Ireland. Three or four times a year, they send out appeal letters to its small, but steadily growing, group of Irish friends and supporters. These people are wonderfully loyal supporters and, the more I hear about them, the more I discover what genuinely good people they are. Many of them cannot afford to give very much money but all, without exception, are uncommonly generous with what they give and they are generous too with their letters and messages of encouragement and support to the staff and the field workers of Refugee Trust.

Part of the reason for this wonderful sense of commitment and involvement is because Refugee Trust always goes out of its way to acknowledge their support by sending 'Thank you' letters in appreciation of every donation received. But these are no ordinary thank you letters. Refugee Trust invests a considerable amount of time, money and effort in making sure that their 'Thank you' letters are an absolute treasure to receive. To give you a better insight into how genuine their 'Thank you' letters can be, first I must show you the appeal letter that generated a very high response. Everybody who made a donation received a very sincere 'Thank you' letter.

Name
Address

Easter 2003

Dear personalised name

... and Brother Tom is building houses in Rwanda

In 1992, three hundred thousand Tutsis were killed in the Bugesera district
of Rwanda. Two years later, the genocide of 1994 left many districts in
Bugesera with a horrifying death total of 90%. Three years ago, the
drought hit Bugesera and with it came more misery and untold hardships
for these very unfortunate people.

> Living in the shadow of history, the survivors and returned refugees
> have struggled to build a peaceful community. And since just
> before last Christmas, Brother Tom O' Grady O.H. has made it his
> mission in life to live among these people and help them to build
> houses for their families.

The houses are for child-headed households, where the head of the
household is a child, often no older than ... 14 ... 15 ... 16 years of age.
They are building a future for their younger brothers and sisters. And they
are building it with their bare hands.

> They are the most wonderful workers in the world. Their spirit of
> co-operation is one of the most uplifting experiences you could ever
> encounter. When one family finishes their own house, they join
> other neighbouring families to try and finish their homes before the
> rainy season starts. **It's like the old harvest thrashing days in
> Ireland with everybody lending a hand.**

These are simple houses and they are built under the careful supervision,
guidance and training of the Refugee Trust Construction Engineer. Simple,
but very effective! Each house costs €683 to build. We've already built
150 of them. We're in the process of building 400 more. We're trying to
finish them before the rainy season and the high winds begin, but we've
run out of money.

You may wonder how on earth can you build a house for an entire family
of children for little more than the cost of one month's rent on a 1-bedroom
apartment in Ireland. **Here's how we do it...**

Item	Unit Cost	Quantity	Total Cost	
Wooden doors	24	2	48	These are simple, modest four-roomed houses (two bedrooms, living room and kitchen with latrine and water supply in their yard). The essential supply of water is a huge challenge and the children have encountered difficulties in the building process, due to lack of water to mix the brick material for their new homes. Every drop of water used is very precious. They've had no real rain up to now.
Wooden Windows	17	4	68	
Iron Sheets	10	36	360	
Ridges	5	6	30	
Nails	2.4	8kg	19	
Hoop Irons	2	3Kg	6	
Timber	2.4	30	72	
Local Technician	80	1	80	
Total cost of a family house			€683	

These children have absolutely nothing or no one to assist them. The child-headed households and their dependants are all unable to read or write. They have no social facilities whatsoever. But by providing them with trade skills in carpentry and construction... **block by block, their future is built.**

It's so exciting to see the joy on the faces of the children as they occupy their own newly built, and self-built, homes.

Unfortunately, Refugee Trust is restricted in what we can provide for them by way of furniture. In fact, most of the 150 newly-built houses are empty save for a few pots and pans for cooking and a mat for sleeping on. In time, when we have more funds available to us, we hope to set up a small furniture workshop where we will teach the children how to make their own furniture, bed-linen and clothing.

But right now, Brother Tom's priority is on building the houses to protect and shelter as many orphan children as possible.

Although Tom is well past the age when most of us would have retired, he's **building ... building ... building homes as urgently and as fast as he possibly can.** He's 400 more homes to complete. But now, he's run out of money.

Please, will you share a little of your wealth to assist Brother Tom to give these children a start with a home of their own. Please!

Yours sincerely

_____ , Chief Executive - Refugee Trust

PS: Although he will never let anybody say it, Brother Tom is a remarkable Irish man. All his life, he has worked for the poor, the blind, the sick and the oppressed. More recently, 1992 - 1998, he was based in the city of Sarajevo all throughout the most horrendous years that the people of that city ever experienced. At the end of the war, the President of Sarajevo, Prof. Dr. Midhat Haracic, proclaimed Brother Tom an honorary citizen of Sarajevo, a rare title to be given to a non-Bosnian person. Although he was seriously ill at the end of the blockade of Sarajevo and had to be air-lifted back to Ireland ... **Brother Tom is now building houses in Rwanda.**

Did you note how carefully the letter shows you how much it costs to build a house (that's the I = Interest element of the AIDA formula)? Note also the little information box at the end that gives you more information about this fascinating man 'Brother Tom' (that's part of the D = Desire element of AIDA).

The letter was accompanied with a full-page donation form, which is reproduced in the next page for your information. In addition, it included a simple, but colourful little card showing a picture of the children making mud bricks to build their homes. The card repeated, yet again, the interesting 'Brother Tom' details that feature in the information box at the end of the letter. All in all, this is a very hard working pack where the core message is presented in the letter and then repeated in different places in the other items that make up the total pack.

On the next page, you will find a reproduction of the full A4-size donation that accompanied the "Brother Tom" appeal letter. It includes the eye-catching story of *'One Man's Determination'*. The reason why this story features here is to remind all the friends and supporters – at the time they are filling in this form – what a wonderful cause, and what a genuinely remarkable man they are supporting. In passing, may I mention to you that the story itself follows the AIDA formula.

And then, immediately following, on page 230, you'll find the *'Thank you'* letter that was sent out to everyone who responded to the appeal.

"Raise High The Roofbeams, Carpenters"
Easter is a time for building on faith
... block by block, Brother Tom is helping children to build houses in Rwanda.

Refugee Trust Easter Appeal

One Man's Determination

Please, will you share a little of your wealth to assist Brother Tom to give these children a start with a home of their own.

Yes, I will help Refugee Trust's work to build homes for child-families in Rwanda. Please find enclosed my donation of:

☐ **€20** will cover the cost of nails for one house
☐ **€48** will cover the cost of 2 wooden doors for one house
☐ **€68** will cover the cost of wooden windows for one house
☐ **€80** will cover the cost of a local technician to help the children to build their house
☐ **€683** will cover the cost of an entire house built by the children with our help - a home!
☐ **€6,830** will cover the cost of ten houses - 10 homes!
☐ **Other Donation €**

Remember, every donation, no matter how small it is, will help us to build a future for these children.

The Standard Name and Address details of the Donation form featured here

'He worked with our people making no distinction about our nationalities and for that he is loved and respected by all. This is why I have great privilege in proclaiming him as an honorary citizen of Sarajevo.

Brother Thomas is respected everywhere for his honesty, dynamism and his professional diplomatic skills in managing projects for senior citizens, traumatised children, the blind and the mentally handicapped. He had multi-disciplinary teams working on the front lines of the conflict through the most dangerous times.

Not only did he restore hospitals, TB Clinics, Psychiatric Homes, Medical Clinics, Displacement Centres and the parish churches in Ilijas and Gorazde, but by his sheer determination and insistence he arranged for professional staff to be trained in Ireland and for professors and doctors and nurses to come here from the United States, Ireland and Great Britain.

He also ensured that the collective centre in Lukavica received maximum material aid during severe winters. This title of honorary citizen has been widely acclaimed both on newspapers and TV. The people of Sarajevo, and particularly those families whose lives have been touched by Refugee Trust Programmes and the generosity of people of Ireland proclaim Brother Thomas as their special ambassador of peace at home and abroad.

Dr Haracic, President of Sarajevo Canton in a letter read at the cabinet table in the presence of the Federal Ministries and the Cantonal Ministries of Sarajevo.

Not surprisingly, the sacrifices, pressure and constant dangers of working in Sarajevo took a serious toil on Brother Tom's Health. At the end of the siege he had to be air-lifted back to Ireland and rushed to hospital here. Tom is no longer a young man. And many of us in Refugee Trust feared greatly for his life at the time.

But we need not have feared. No! Never! Because Tom is a determined man with a mission.

A few months ago he packed his bags and set off for Rwanda. Today, as you are reading this urgent appeal letter, Brother Tom is building houses.

Tom needs all the help and support we can give him.

Any gift during the tax year of €254, or more, from an Irish resident qualifies **Refugee Trust Ireland** for a Tax Refund. This means: A/ If you are a PAYE earner, at the end of the tax year the Revenue Commissioners give the refund directly to Refugee Trust. B/ If you are self-assessed or if the donation comes from a business account, you can reclaim the tax you have already paid on your gift. Either way, at no extra cost to you, a gift of €254 in a tax year is worth an extra €50+ to Refugee Trust Ireland if you pay tax at the standard rate of 20%, or an extra €100+ if you are on the higher rate. **Think of how many extra homes we can build with this extra money.**

Name
Address

Date

Dear personalised name

It brings out goodness and happiness in everyone

I'm writing to thank you for your generous response to our Easter Appeal
for funds to help Brother Tom build houses for the children of Bugesera in
Rwanda. He's asked me to tell you that it's a wonderful feeling for him to
know that he has a good friend like you at his side.

> In recent weeks many of our friends and supporters have contacted
> us to ask how they can take a more active part in the building work
> that Brother Tom is doing. Some are organising coffee mornings
> and fund raising events of their own to help him to build a house for
> these children on behalf of their family or neighbourhood.

Others wonder how a man of Tom's advanced age can keep going,
particularly after his emergency airlift to hospital from Sarajevo just a few
short years ago. At that time many of us thought that we had lost a good
friend, but we underestimated Tom's determination.

> You see, as Tom constantly reminds us… 'There is so much work
> to be done, so much good that each and every one of us can do in
> our life, and so many hungry people depending on us to do it now!'

Tom is deeply touched by your support and concern. He always believes
that something very special happens when a group of friends share their
resources to create a better future for less well off children. It brings out
goodness and happiness in everyone. And you are one of those special
friends.

I hope that by sharing these words with you I can give you a deeper
understanding of how much Brother Tom and everyone here in Refugee
Trust appreciates your help and support.

Yours sincerely

_____

Chief Executive - Refugee Trust International

Everybody who responded to the *'Brother Tom'* appeal received this warm and very personal thank you letter. Refugee Trust, and Brother Tom himself, wanted everyone to know how much they genuinely appreciated their friendship and support.

Now I don't know about you, but I would certainly appreciate being sent a *'Thank you'* letter like this. It would make me feel that I *'belong'* to a very special group of friends!

Here's another example of a simple little *'Thank you'* letter that I received from a client of mine. I certainly appreciated receiving this letter and, again, it created that all-important *'I belong'* feeling. The letter is definitely a 'buying friendship' letter, but the sense of *'I belong'* that it creates is pure salesmanship. That's why it fits the genre of what I term a 'sales' thank-you letter.

Dear Robert

I've just signed off our year-end accounts with our auditors and the bottom line is that we have had another excellent year trading.

I'm writing to you to thank you for all the good work that you have done for us over the past year. I very much appreciate it.

Sometimes amid the hustle and bustle of day-to-day business activity it can be so easy for us to forget how much of our success we owe to our suppliers like you.

You are an important part of our team and, Robert, it's good to know that we have people like you – people that we can depend on – on our side.

We're all looking forward to working with you in the future and may I thank you again for your important contribution to our success.

Yours sincerely

John Murphy
Chief Executive

Short, simple and sweet, and while I know that maybe hundreds of other of the company's suppliers received this letter as well, this didn't in any way diminish my satisfaction of receiving this *'Thank you'* letter. It made me feel *'I belong'*.

Never underestimate the friendship-winning power of a personal *'Thank you'* letter like this. A *'Thank you'* letter like this can be sent to anyone, including your customers. Here's a few examples of a 'sales thank you' letter that, with a few modifications, I think just about every one of your customer would enjoy receiving from you.

Dear Mr Jones

At this time of the year, I always make a point of taking some time out from my work schedule to write a little thank you note to valued customers and good friends like you.

> You see, I want you to know that we appreciate you doing your family grocery shopping with us every week.

We're proud of the fact that we have many regular customers like you. If there is ever anything extra that we can do for you, some additional item that you'd like us to stock or some extra service that will make your shopping experience with us more enjoyable, please let me know.

> Just ask one of our shop assistants to call me any time you are doing your shopping here and I'll be delighted to come down and talk to you about it.

In the meantime, thank you for shopping with us, it's good to know that we have customers like you.

Yours sincerely

Tom Murphy
Manager

Dear Mrs McEvoy

I'm writing to thank you for being a valued customer of ours.

On behalf of all of us in XYZ Company, I'd like you to know that we appreciate your custom and we are looking forward to being of service to you for many more years into the future.

If you ever have any ideas or suggestions that you'd like to make about how we can improve our service to you, please let me know.

> My direct-line telephone number is **12345678** and, if for any reason I'm away from my desk when you call, my secretary, Mary Moore, will pass on your message to me and I'll call you back without fail.

In the meantime may I thank you again for your custom and support. We value customers like you.

Yours sincerely

Bobby Smith
Chief Executive

Thank you letters like these fit into the category of what I call **'buying'** letters. But they are also true sales letters.

Remember, sometimes we're all so busy selling our products and services that we forget that we should be buyers too. And what we should set out to buy is our customers' ongoing loyalty and support. The simple thank you letter, as the heading on the Brother Tom letter so aptly puts it ... *'brings out happiness and goodness in everyone'*. And what better customers can you have than happy customers!

SUMMARY OF CHAPTER 24:
HERE'S WHAT YOU SAY AND HOW YOU SAY IT

☐ *'Thank you'* letters are an important part of the sales process and yet relatively few companies that I've come across are prepared to invest time and money in sending out what they consider to be 'unnecessary' letters like these to their valued customers.

☐ Charities have been harnessing the power of *'Thank you'* letters for years, because they know that it strengthens the bond between their organisation and their donors. If these letters work for charitable organisations that have to keep a very careful eye on their overhead expenses, then surely they must work for commercial enterprises as well.

☐ The more personal you can make the tone of your *'Thank you'* letter, the more it will be appreciated and valued by the recipients. Opt for sincerity rather than effusion in your *'Thank you'* message and avoid going over the top.

☐ An obviously-photocopied *'Thank you'* letter, or the same letter used year after year, will not have the desired effect on your readers. Invest a bit of time in making your *'Thank you'* message interesting and fresh, and your investment will certainly pay dividends in the number of extra friends that you make and in the enhanced sense of *'I belong'* that you generate among the most important people in your business ... your loyal customers.

25. BRINGING EVERYTHING TOGETHER

> 'They sought it with thimbles, they sought it with care;
> They pursued it with folks and with hope;
> They threatened its life with a railway-share;
> They charmed it with smiles and soap.'
> Lewis Carroll, *The Hunting of the Snark* (1876).

When I was setting up my own copywriter company, and there was very little money to spare for promoting and advertising my services, I developed a low-budget marketing campaign that worked wonders for me. So good was the response that the campaign received a Special Award from the European Direct Marketing Association in Brussels.

The promotional piece was simplicity in itself, and everything featured on a single A4 sheet of paper that contained two mini sales letters. Everybody who received this sheet of paper was invited to compare the two letters and see whether they could identify why Letter A was, in my view, a better sales letter than Letter B.

I offered no prizes to the winners, but you would not believe how much attention this single A4 page captured in the marketplace both in Ireland and overseas. All kinds of people rang me and faxed me (that was in pre-email days) with what they considered to be the correct answers to my little teaser. I even got people calling into my office, wanting to know whether they were the first, because somehow or other they had figured out that there was a prize for the person with the first correct answers. The response was quite incredible.

But the one that I will always remember was the excited voice on the telephone of a very senior bank official who proudly informed me, *'Robert, I've found 15 reasons why Letter A is better than Letter B. Do I get a special prize?'*.

Fifteen reasons! Believe you me, there are not 15 reasons. There are **six** reasons. And if you really want to stretch your imagination, you'll find seven! To anybody who has read this book, you'll find this little test of skills very straightforward because all six (actually, there's seven) reasons have been carefully covered and explained throughout the various chapters of this book of mine. I've given you the answers at the end of the chapter. I'd like to invite you to have a go and see if you can spot the six reasons why Letter A is a better sales letter than Letter B.

The response that I got to this little A4 promotional sheet was exceptionally high. In addition to the seven reasons outlined at the end of the chapter, there is a number of strategic reasons why this campaign of mine, using two mini sales letters, was such an international award winning success.

You see, these miniscule sales letters applied just about every trick in the direct marketing copywriter's book to capture A = Attention, generate I = Interest, create D = Desire and encourage A = Action on the part of the readers. And the book that I'm referring to is, of course, this book that you are now holding in your hands.

In a few moments, we'll bring it all together on a chapter-by-chapter basis and see how the guidelines contained in each chapter build up, layer upon layer, into a successful sales letter strategy. But before we do, look carefully at the two letters on the next page and see whether you can work out the seven reasons why Letter A is a better sales letter than Letter B.

Try it! You'll find the answers in the Appendix on page 251.

Robert Hayes-McCoy

Copywriter, invites you to test your writing communication skills ... by giving
six reasons (actually, there's seven) why letter "A" below, is a better sales letter than letter 'B'.

LETTER A	LETTER B
Dear reader	Dear reader
It's hard to know how to write a good Direct Marketing letter.	It's hard to know how to write a good Direct Marketing letter.
That's why professional direct marketing copywriters are a relatively rare breed ... not just in Ireland, **but all over the world**.	That's why professional direct marketing copywriters are a relatively rare breed ... not just in Ireland, but all over the world. And yet, time and time again it can be proven that the letter is the most important item in your mail pack. In many ways, the letter is the voice of your sales rep and the glossy brochure is the pin stripe suit he is wearing.
And yet, time and time again it can be proven that the letter is the most important item in your mail pack. In many ways, the letter is the voice of your sales rep and the glossy brochure is the pin-stripe suit he is wearing.	
Each has an important role to play in the sales process. But if the voice is not right, no amount of expensive clothing will ever successfully cover for a weak sales letter.	Each has an important role to play in the sales process. But if the voice is not right no amount of expensive clothing will ever successfully cover for a weak sales letter. It's not just what you say, but how you say it ... and where you should increase the tempo (and where you should slow down) that makes the all-important difference between a good sales rep and a mediocre one. That's why investing €390 in getting Robert Hayes-McCoy Consultants to write your next Direct Marketing Sales letter could be the most cost-effective part of your entire mailing pack.
It's not just what you say, but how you say it ... and where you should increase the tempo (and where you should **slow down**) that makes the all-important difference between a good sales rep and a mediocre one.	
That's why investing **€390** in getting Robert Hayes-McCoy Consultants to write your next Direct Marketing Sales letter could be the most cost-effective part of your entire mailing pack.	
Simply call me on **01-260 39 49** and I'll be delighted to write your next Direct Marketing letter for you.	Simply call me on 01-260 39 49 and I'll be delighted to write your next Direct Marketing letter for you.
Kind regards	Kind regards
[signature]	*Robert Hayes-McCoy*
Robert Hayes-McCoy	Robert Hayes-McCoy
PS: Why not call me at that number now?	PS: Why not call me at that number now?

WHAT THEY SAY ABOUT ROBERT HAYES-M^{c}COY'S COPYWRITING

'Robert Hayes-McCoy writes great business letters – the kind of letters people like to receive.'
Murray Raphel (USA), Author: The Great Brain Robbery.
... 'Congratulations on creating one of the most original and memorable direct mail campaigns I have seen in forty years of opening business envelopes.'
Stan Rapp (USA), Author: Beyond Maximarketing.
... 'Mr Hayes-McCoy's copy has a quality largely ignored by copywriters, one drawn to my attention by David Ogilvy over dinner one evening ... charm and character'.
Drayton Bird (UK), Author: Commonsense Direct Marketing.

☎ **+353- 1-260 39 49** ☎

CHAPTERS 1 & 2

In the opening chapters of this book, I introduced you to a number of magic words. I explained to you that these are the 'hidden persuaders', as it were and I encouraged you, if at all possible, to try and use a magic word in your opening paragraph, or in your headline. I explained to you that the most powerful magic word of all is the platinum word, 'You' (or any variation of the word 'you': 'yours', 'you're', 'yourself', etc).

Now have a look again at my award-winning mini-letter promotional piece on page 236. It's a single sheet of A4 paper. And right up there, at the very top, you'll find that I use the platinum word twice in the headline '… invites **you** to test **your** skills …'.

And, in the opening paragraph of my mini sales letter, I use the magic words 'how to'.

Sales Letter Writer's checklist # 1	Check to see whether you can use a magic word in your opening paragraph.

CHAPTER 3

In addition to introducing you to the platinum magic word in **Chapter 3**, I encouraged you always to do a 'U-count' before you finally sign off on your draft sales letter. I explained to you that you need to spread the 'Yous' across your letter, because the wider your spread of 'Yous', the more chance you have of holding on to your readers' attention all throughout your letter.

That's one of the reasons that I took such care to have two 'Yous' in my introduction to my mini letters. I relied on the attention-capturing powers of the opening two paragraphs, coupled with the magic words 'how to', to carry the reader through to the third paragraph of my mini letter. And then, in the third, fifth, sixth and seventh paragraphs of Letter A, I took great care to ensure that I had – at minimum two 'You's' in every paragraph. And, for added good measure, I finished my letter on the platinum word 'You'.

Sales Letter Writer's checklist # 2	Do a U-count.

CHAPTER 4

In **Chapter Four**, I introduced a note of caution about overusing the magic words. And I explained to you that with the exception of the platinum magic word 'You', you should considerably reduce your use of magic words in the remainder of your sales letter on the basis that: *'Magic dies young!'*.

If you look at my mini sales letter, you'll see that I follow this advice carefully. Other than the opening paragraph, the only other place that you'll find a magic word in my mini sales letter is in the PS, where the very last word is *'now'*.

Sales Letter Writer's checklist # 3	Check that you haven't gone over the top with your use of magic words.

CHAPTER 5

Here, I introduced you to the 'Lady in Red' and I reiterated how important it is for you to get your opening paragraph right.

In this mini letter promotion of mine, I found myself confronted with an interesting question, which opening paragraph should I concentrate on getting right: The opening introduction at the top of the page or the opening paragraph in the mini letter itself?

Actually, there isn't any question about it … it's the **opening** paragraph – the very first thing that the reader will read – that is of paramount importance. So I presented my readers with an interesting invitation/challenge in the real opening paragraph in this promotional piece. **And,** just to be on the safe side, I created an interesting little two-liner as the opening paragraph of the mini letter itself.

Sales Letter Writer's checklist # 4	Check that your opening paragraph is interesting for your readers.

CHAPTER 6

Chapter Six explains the concept of editing from the top. If your letter has an uninteresting opening paragraph, or if you find that your finished draft is too long and needs to be knocked down to size, you should edit from the top.

In my mini sales letter, I had an unusually small amount of space to work in. As you can see, I successfully managed to capture everything that I wanted to say within this challenging amount of space. Needless to say, this is the result of repeated, and repeated, and repeated editing from the top.

Sales Letter Writer's checklist # 5	Always apply the 'edit from the top' formula to see whether you can improve your draft letter.

CHAPTER 7

In **Chapter Seven**, I explained the importance of good testimonials to you. As it so happened, I was very lucky to have some excellent testimonials for my work. They were so good, that I gave them pride of place in a special box of their own at the bottom of my A4 page.

Sales Letter Writer's checklist # 6	If you have a good testimonial, see whether you can you use it.

CHAPTER 8

Getting the tone of your letter right. In this chapter, I explained to you that, if you want to capture and hold your readers' attention, you must make your letter interesting 'to your readers'. My entire strategy in this promotional piece is to create an interesting little game for my readers to play.

Sales Letter Writer's checklist # 7	Check that you've written your entire letter in an interesting and lively tone.

CHAPTERS 9 & 10

In these two chapters, I highlighted the importance of keeping your sentences and your paragraphs short and 'easy on the eye' to read. This is an integral part of the *'compare these two letters'* game. The reader can see at a glance how Letter B suffers from overlong paragraphs.

Sales Letter Writer's checklist # 8	Check that your sentences and paragraphs are not too long.

CHAPTER 11

In this chapter, I explained to you that the appearance of your letter is very important. I explained about the value of a PS and I advised you to use a clear and legible blue-ink signature. You'll notice that my two mini letters open with the salutation, *'Dear Reader'*. When I was sending out these promotional pages to my target group, I took great care to personalise my two mini letters. And, as I've already mentioned to you, I personally signed Letter A, so that it would contrast sharply with the computer-produced signature of Letter B.

Sales Letter Writer's checklist # 9	Check for use of personalisation and a legible signature.

CHAPTER 12

In this chapter, I mentioned that, if you have a good story to tell about your product or service, you should not be afraid of using more than one page in your sales letter. In my mini-letter promotion, I actually had a very long story to tell – a story that if I tried to put words to it all would definitely have run into two pages. But I decided to use the contrasting appearance of my two letters to tell the story for me. By inviting my readers to see whether they could spot the six differences between the two mini letters, I was able to cut down on the number of words I used and put my sales proposition to them without my letter running over to a second page.

Sales Letter Writer's checklist # 10	If your letter runs to two pages, check that you have ended your first page in mid-sentence.

CHAPTER 13

This is the chapter with the catchy heading, *'Money is shortsighted'*. Unfortunately, for space reasons, I couldn't use a larger type size in my two mini letters. You see, had I gone larger, I wouldn't have been able to position the two letters beside each other on the A4 page which would have defeated the whole purpose of my *'spot the difference'* game strategy.

To achieve this objective, I had to settle for a very small 8 point type size. Needless to say, this was a real worry to me when I was sending out my promotional piece. I was genuinely worried that, because of the very small type size that I was using, I would lose many of my readers. Indeed, had the *'spot the difference'* game not been interesting enough to hold their attention, I think I would have lost them. I admit, this was a gamble on my part, but luckily enough it paid off with very handsome dividends. However, a small type size like this is not something that I would recommend lightly to anyone to use.

Sales Letter Writer's checklist # 11	Check to see whether it is possible for you to use a larger type size.

CHAPTER 14

In this chapter, I explained to you the problems that can be encountered with paragraph spacing and how each paragraph space creates a 'hole' in your sales letter where you might 'leak' readers. I also explained to you that your computer software programme might simply vary the spaces between the words of your text in its machinations to create justified endings to your text.

Variable spacing between words makes for lumpy cumbersome reading, which can have a negative effect on your sales letter. In my mini letter promotional sheet, I used both justified and unjustified text in my contrasting letters and I also used smaller paragraph spacing in Letter A. However, because I was using a very small 8 point type size in both mini letters, I really didn't expect many of my readers to spot the difference in paragraph spacing. That's why I merely referred to this last as an aside: *'Actually, there's seven differences ...'*.

Sales Letter Writer's checklist # 12	Check that you are using unjustified endings in preference to justified endings, especially if you are using a large font size.

CHAPTER 15

This is the chapter that refers to paragraph transitions and connectors. Paragraph spaces, as mentioned above, are 'holes' where you may 'leak' readers. You'll notice that the paragraphs in my mini letters all start with rapid forward-moving transitional words: *'That's why'* ... *'And yet'* ... *'Each has'* ... *'It's not just'* ... etc. As you can see, I'm working very hard within my mini letter to keep my readers reading to the end of my letter.

Sales Letter Writer's checklist # 13	Check that the transition between paragraphs is as fast flowing and as smooth as possible.

CHAPTER 16

This is the chapter where wise old Aristotle tells us that *'Style to be good must be clear'*. In my mini letter, I've kept everything as clear as possible. I've used no unusual words and, in my example of how a good sales letter works, I've used a simple analogy that just about everybody will have no difficulty relating to: *'In many ways, the letter is the voice of your sales rep and the glossy brochure is the pin stripe suit he is wearing'*. Of course, I could have come up with a more impressive-sounding example but, in the interests of achieving maximum clarity, I decided to keep everything as down-to-earth and as clear as possible.

Sales Letter Writer's checklist # 14	Check your letter for jargon or unusual words that your readers may not understand and replace them with more commonly-used words.

CHAPTERS 17 & 18

In this chapter, you are introduced to the lovely AIDA: A = Attention, I = Interest, D = Desire and A = Action. Everything about my mini letter promotional sheet is designed to capture my readers' attention right from the outset. The I = Interest factor is in the detail of having fun testing your skills by comparing the two letters and spotting the difference. It's also in the mini letter itself, as I briefly (but choosing my words and example very carefully) explain to my readers how difficult it is to write a sales letter. The D = Desire factor is achieved when, after explaining to my readers that it's far more difficult than you might think to write a good sales letter, I then immediately go on to introduce them to a remarkably easy way out … just ask me to write it for you. The A = Action factor is in the last paragraph and in the PS of my mini letter, where I invite them to call me and I tell them that I'll be delighted to write their next letter for them if they call me … now! You'll notice that I also spell out my fees in my mini letter and this, I was told by just about everybody who contacted me, made it even easier for my readers to decide whether or not to use my services.

Sales Letter Writer's checklist # 15	Check that your letter follows the AIDA formula.

CHAPTER 19

This is the chapter that alerts you to the fact that many people in our society have difficulties with reading and writing, so you should try to keep everything as simple and as easy to understand as possible. While I was unable (for space reasons which I have explained above) to use a large easy-to-read font size in my mini letter, as you can see I did work very hard to use easily-understood words throughout. I also touched a very sensitive button in the opening paragraph of my mini letter: *'It's hard to know how to write a good Direct Marketing letter'*. I know for a fact that some of the people who contacted me as a result of receiving this promotional sheet from me, and who subsequently commissioned me to write their sales letters for them, identified very closely with the sentiments expressed in this opening paragraph of mine.

Sales Letter Writer's checklist # 16	Check that you are not using technical terminology that some of your readers' may not understand.

CHAPTER 20

This is the chapter where you had fun *'Picturing this!'*. You will recall that I advised you to use word-pictures to explain technical or difficult concepts. In my mini letter, I explained how crucial a good sales letter is to the success of every direct mail pack by painting that nice cosy little word-picture: *'In many ways, the letter is the voice of your sales rep and the glossy brochure is the pin stripe suit he is wearing'*.

Sales Letter Writer's checklist # 17	Check that your letter is not getting bogged down in too many technical details – if it is, try using word-pictures to make things clearer.

CHAPTER 21

In this chapter, I explained to you that you should decide from the outset what exactly you want your sales letter to achieve. Keep it simple: the clearer your objective, the easier it will be for you to write your letter. In my mini letter, my objective was to tell my readers that they should contact me if they want a sales letter written. I give them my telephone number and invite them to call me. I tell them that I'll be delighted to hear from them and, for added impact, I repeat my telephone number in big bold letters at the very bottom of the page.

Sales Letter Writer's checklist # 18	Check to see that your letter clearly tells your readers what you want them to do.

CHAPTER 22

This is the chapter where I set down my Seven Strategic Rules for Success. Have a look at the list below and I think you'll find that my mini letter promotional sheet complies with them all.

1. Know your key selling points.
2. Address your sales message correctly.
3. Avoid using the dreaded *'Dear Sir/Madam'* salutation.
4. Make the appearance of your letter appropriate to your offer.
5. Answer the WI-IFM question for your readers.
6. KISS – Keep it Simple, Stupid!
7. Make it easy for your readers to respond to you.

Sales Letter Writer's checklist # 19	Check that you are not – definitely not – using a *'Dear Sir/Madam'* salutation.

CHAPTER 23

This is the mysterious stranger chapter: *'Never Sell To A Stranger'*. Do you remember when I was showing you how Customer Relationship Marketing (CRM) worked, I explained to you the power of the follow-up letter? Well, in my mini letter promotional sheet, you will see the power of the follow-up letter in live action on a single sheet. This, I believe played a very important part in the huge success of this mini letter promotion. You see, there are not very many promotions where your readers will carefully read every single word you write – **not once, but twice!** By inviting my readers to compare two identical sales letters presented to them on a single sheet of paper, in effect I was reaping the benefits of them reading two sales letters from me at the same time. In effect, I was sending them an introduction letter and a follow-up reminder letter on the same sheet.

Sales Letter Writer's checklist # 20	Check that you have kept the door open for a possible follow-up reminder letter. For example, don't say foolish things like: 'If I don't hear from you, I'll take it that you are not interested and I won't contact you again'.

YOUR HANDY CHECKLIST FOR WRITING A VERY PERSUASIVE SALES LETTER

✓	1.	Yes!	I've used a magic word in my opening paragraph.
✓	2.	Yes!	I've done a U-count.
✓	3.	Yes!	I haven't gone over the top with my use of magic words in the rest of my letter.
✓	4.	Yes!	**For my readers,** my opening paragraph is definitely interesting.
✓	5.	Yes!	I've edited from the top to see whether I can strengthen my sales letter
✓	6.	Yes!	I've checked to see whether I have a good testimonial to use in my letter.
✓	7.	Yes!	I've double-checked to confirm that my **entire** letter is an easy read.
✓	8.	Yes!	My sentences and paragraphs are not too long.
✓	9.	Yes!	I've used the correct personalisation and a legible signature.
✓	10.	Yes!	Where my letter runs to two pages, I've checked that page 1 ends in mid-sentence.
✓	11.	Yes!	I've looked to see whether it is possible for me to use a larger type size.
✓	12.	Yes!	I'm using unjustified endings in my text.
✓	13.	Yes!	I've made my paragraphs transitions as fast-flowing and as smooth as possible.
✓	14.	Yes!	I'm not using any jargon that my readers may not understand.
✓	15.	Yes!	My letter follows the AIDA formula.
✓	16.	Yes!	I'm not talking down to my readers by using uncommonly used words.
✓	17.	Yes!	I'm not bogging down my readers with too many tedious technical details.
✓	18.	Yes!	My letter clearly tells my readers what I want them to do.
✓	19.	Yes!	I'm not – **definitely not** – using a *'Dear Sir/Madam'* salutation to my good customers.
✓	20.	Yes!	I have kept the door open for a possible follow-up reminder letter.

THANK YOU!

Thank you for reading my book! In my opening introduction, I promised you that by the time you reached the end of it – which is now – you would be armed with all the information you need to write really great sales letters.

Next time you have a sales letter to write, follow the rules and strategies outlined in this book. Use the handy checklist on page 246 to ensure that nothing is omitted and you should have no worries – no worries at all – about the effectiveness of your sales letter. Believe me, it will be one of the most persuasive sales letters you've ever written!

Since I'm determined to conclude with the most important word of all in the sales letter writer's tool kit, I'd like you to know that I've now shared much of what I know about writing award-winning sales letter with you.

At this stage, it's over to… **YOU!**

APPENDIX: LETTER A *VS* LETTER B: ANSWERS

Before we start, can I point out to you that both letters are identical insofar as they both say exactly the same thing. Every single word that is used in Letter A is replicated in Letter B and no additional words are added.

1. The first one is easy. I carefully wrote my signature in blue ink on Letter A with a fountain pen on every single sheet that I sent out. It took me ages, but it was well worth every minute of the time I invested in it. Remember, a clear legible blue-ink signature will pull a far better response to your sales letter than an obviously 'computerised script' signature or an illegible squiggle.

2. Letter A is written in a serif type font, while letter B is written in a san-serif type font. I used Times New Roman in Letter A while I used Arial in Letter B. Although Times New Roman is a slightly old-fashioned-looking type font, it makes for almost effortless reading. Incidentally, although I'm using an 8 pt font size in both letters, you can see immediately that Arial is inherently a larger size font than Times New Roman.

3. Letter A has unjustified endings to the lines of text while Letter B has justified endings. When my computer software is instructed to create justified endings, it achieves its task by varying the size of the spaces between individual words. In small font sizes, these space variations between the words are not so noticeable but, as your font size gets bigger, you'll notice them immediately and you'll find that it is distracting your eyes, and your attention, away from what is being said in the text. Look closely at Letter B and you'll see the variable space sizes between some of the words.

4. Letter A has shorter paragraphs than Letter B. Just look at paragraph 3 of Letter B. It **looks**, and it is, far too long, which makes it very difficult for the reader to concentrate on.

5. Letter A uses indented paragraphs to give the reader's eye a short resting-point every now and again. This makes the letter **look** like a much more relaxed read than Letter B. It's more inviting! By the way, because these are mini letters and I'm using (for space reasons alone) a very small 8 pt font size in each, you don't really notice that I've carefully indented **both sides** of each of the three indented paragraphs in Letter A. A double-sided indentation, as opposed to the more conventional 'indent on the left side only' gives a more

balanced appearance to your indented paragraphs that is more pleasing to the reader's eye. Beware of overdoing the size of the indent. If you indent by too much, you'll disrupt the natural movement of the reader's eye and it will create a jumpy effect in the easy forward-moving momentum of your sales letter. You will recall what I mentioned to you in a previous chapter – I don't want the reader to pause for too long between the paragraphs for fear that I might lose them, so I only use a small indentation.

6. Letter A also uses **'bold face'** type in four different places throughout the letter. This gives the overall appearance of the letter a little lift every now and again and makes it more vibrant and interesting to look at. Bold face type is slightly slower to read than normal type and you'll notice that I've deliberately used bold face type on the words **'slow down'**.

7. If you have managed to get all six correct answers so far, well done! Now, how about the seventh? Did you manage to spot it? Most of the recipients of this little teaser page wouldn't have had a breeze what to look out for. But you, the readers of my book, will have probably noticed the different in paragraph spacing between the two letters. The font size in both letters is 8 point but, in Letter A, I've carefully reduced the spaces between the paragraphs by 50% down to 4 point. Reducing the spaces between the paragraphs to approximately half the size of the font used in the text helps to speed up the rhythm of the letter and made it a faster read. The faster your readers can read your sales letters, the more information they will absorb and retain.

Special Thanks

I'd like to take this opportunity to say a special word of thanks to my wonderful wife, Anne, whose work and time input into the creation and development of this book was absolutely awesome.

And, of course, I must thank my long-suffering children: Declan, Stephen and Dermot for tolerating me in bemused silence as I wandered about the house talking aloud to myself in my never-ending quest to write the way I talk.

My sincere thanks must go my good friend and adviser, Kieran Devenish, who spent weeks proofing, correcting and offering me invaluable suggestions on how to improve this book.

So many generous people helped me with advice and – best of all – with permission to use their own creative material and ideas in this book, it's impossible for me to mention you all by name. But I think you know who you are and I'd like you to know that I am very grateful to each and every one of you.

My friend Alastair Tempest, Director General of the European Direct Marketing Association (FEDMA) deserves special mention. Sincere thanks must also go to Refugee Trust, Peter Mercier, Peter Manahan and to Olwen Kelleghan for allowing me to share their very special letters with you.

And a very big thank you must also go to my editor Brian O'Kane of OAK TREE PRESS, who was an absolute pleasure to work with. I couldn't have asked for a better editor.

Thank you everyone.